THE GREAT BOOK OF PUB TRIVIA

Hilarious Pub Quiz & Bar Trivia Questions

Trivia Quiz Books

By
Bill O'Neill

ISBN-13: 978-1978145122

DON'T FORGET YOUR FREE BOOKS

INTRODUCTION

Welcome to *The Great Book of Pub Trivia*! Get ready to dig in to some fun and nostalgic trivia quizzes and that surely will make your mind spin. This book is meant to be fun and can be used by yourself, just reading and testing your skills or it can be used as a fun game with scoring system with your friends and family. Every quiz section have five questions followed by the answers on the next page.

Enough with the boring introduction… let the fun trivia begin!

Quiz 1

1. Japanese carmaker Nissan makes cars models like Almera and Altima. They also make the luxury car brand Infiniti. For advertising, Nissan cars normally use what number, which goes back to how 2 and 3 are said in Japanese?

2. F. Scott Fitzgerald famously wrote The Great Gatsby, and even though it's considered a great work, the book he died writing was considered to be even better. Fitzgerald asked his friend Nathaniel West to finish the book in the event of his death, but unfortunately West died one day after Fitzgerald. This book was recently adapted into a series by Amazon. What is it called?

3. Without Shakespeare, common expressions like sending him packing, all the world's a stage, we have seen better days, wild goose chase, love is blind, all's well that ends well, and the long and short of it wouldn't exist. What other expressions can we thank Shakespeare for?

4. During their heyday, Frank Sinatra, Dean Martin, and Sammy Davis Junior were part of a popular group of famous entertainers who took Las Vegas by storm. Originally, Humphrey Bogart, Errol Flynn, and Nat King Cole were members. What was the name of this group?

5. In which city will you find the point where Germany, France, and Switzerland all meet? The city is right on the Rhine River, and it's home to the Kunstmuseum, which holds Switzerland's largest art collection. You will also find a Gothic cathedral and the Beyeler Foundation there. What is the name of this city?

Answers to Quiz 1

1. 23 because in Japanese, a 2 is pronounced 'ni' and a 3 is pronounced 'san'.

2. The Last Tycoon

3. Green eyed monster, give the devil his due, fair play/foul play

4. The Rat Pack

5. Basel

Quiz 2

1. The earth's crust is made up of plates, and their movements determine the landmarks that occur. These movements are convergent, where plates move towards each other, divergent, where plates pull apart, and transform, where plates grind sideways against each other. What geographic feature occurs at a divergent zone at the earth's surface?

2. Which country doesn't have a rectangular flag? It is bordered by China and India. It is home to the Sherpas, who serve as porters for mountain climbers. It is also part of the Himalayas mountain range, and its capital city is Kathmandu. Name this country.

3. Margaret Hyra is an American actress who is best known for films like Sleepless in Seattle, You've Got Mail, and Kate & Leopold. She was once married to Dennis Quaid, and the last name she uses is actually her grandmother's maiden name. What is her stage name?

4. What name is given to the methods used for making an aircraft hard to detect? It is also called low observable technology, and it is applied to aircraft, ships, submarines, missiles, and satellites to make them less visible to radar and other forms of detection. What is the name of this technology?

5. Which serial killer was also known as 'The Whitechapel Murderer'? He terrorized the Whitechapel district of London in 1888. He killed at least five prostitutes, but he was never captured and remains one of the world's most infamous criminals. What is the name of this famous killer?

Answers to Quiz 2

1. Rift valley

2. Nepal

3. Meg Ryan

4. Stealth Technology

5. Jack the Ripper

Quiz 3

1. This is an American science fiction drama television series which originally aired from September 10, 1993, to May 19, 2002. The series tells the story of FBI special agents Fox Mulder and Dana Scully who investigate unsolved cases involving the paranormal. It was recently rebooted in a 10-episode show, which will be returning in 2018. It also has two movies. What is the name of this TV show?

2. If you were in an Arab country, this item of clothing would be considered dirty because it comes into contact with the floor. If you show the bottom part of it, you would offend people, and if you throw it at someone this is a serious insult. What is this?

3. Which condiment was originally used as a medicine to treat diarrhea? It is a red sauce made from tomatoes, vinegar, and seasonings. The market leader in United States and United Kingdom is Heinz. It is used as an accompaniment to French fries, hamburgers, and hot dogs. What is this condiment?

4. In psychology, what is an anxiety disorder where people experience impulses and unwanted thoughts. People with this disorder also struggle with compulsions and actions they take to try to get rid of the thoughts that place them. Name this illness.

5. What is a high-altitude kingdom located within South Africa? Its capital city is Maseru, and it is ruled by Letsie III. The nation also contains a network of rivers and mountain ranges. It even has a ski resort. What is this nation's name?

Answers to Quiz 3

1. The X-Files

2. Shoes

3. Ketchup

4. Obsessive Compulsive Disorder

5. Lesotho

Quiz 4

1. Walt Disney refused to allow a famous film maker to film at Disneyland in the early 1960s because he had made "that disgusting movie Psycho." This legendary director is known as a pioneer of the suspense genre, with movies like Psycho, The Birds, Rear Window, Vertigo, and Strangers on a Train. He worked closely with Grace Kelly, and is still considered one of the best English directors of all time. What was this film maker's name?

2. Which star sign is born between 23 October – 21 November? These people are led by their own desires, but they are also incredibly resourceful. Famous people under these star signs include Katy Perry, Leonardo DiCaprio, and Bill Gates. They are also known for secrecy and intensity. What is this zodiac sign?

3. This planet is the second from the sun, and it has the longest rotation period of all the planets. According to Wikipedia, "This planet is sometimes called Earth's sister planet because of their similar size, mass, proximity to the Sun, and bulk composition." It is named after the Roman goddess of love and beauty. What is this planet?

4. He is a high-end shoe designer whose highly sought-after products are well-known for their shiny red bottoms. Based in Paris, the eponymous brand now includes men's footwear, handbags, fragrances, and makeup. The brand also recently launched a collection of nude shoes for every skin tone. What is the name of this brand/designer?

5. This wine takes its color from the grape skins, even though it isn't enough color to make it a red wine. It is pink in color and can be made still, semi-sparkling, or sparkling and with a wide range of sweetness. What is the name of this kind of wine?

Answers to Quiz 4

1. Alfred Hitchcock

2. Scorpio

3. Venus

4. Christian Louboutin

5. Rosé

Quiz 5

1. Elizabeth Taylor was married 8 times to 7 different men. She married Conrad 'Nicky' Hilton, founder of the Hilton hotel chain. Next, she married Michael Wilding, Michael Todd, Eddie Fisher, Richard Burton, John Warner, and Larry Fortensky. Which husband did she marry twice and was considered the love of her life?

2. This is an action comedy film based on a 1970s television series of the same name which starred Farrah Fawcett. The film version starred Cameron Diaz, Drew Barrymore, and Lucy Liu as three women who worked as ass-kicking private detective agents. The also starred Bill Murray, and the sequel, Full Throttle, also starred Demi Moore as the villain. What was the name of this movie?

3. This kind of ice tends to coat road surfaces, and even though it is thin and visually transparent, it can cause skidding and road accidents because the road becomes slippery and tires lose their grip easily. It is named for the fact that the road is still visible underneath. What is this kind of ice called?

4. What was the name of the infamous Colombian drug lord and narcoterrorist who was once richest man in the world with a net worth of $30 billion at the height of his empire? At some point, 80% of the cocaine flowing into the US was generated by his cartel. Once called, "The King of Cocaine," he is now the subject of the popular Netflix show Narcos, which is now in its third season. What was his name?

5. What is an Italian cathedral called? This word comes from the Latin word for house, because a cathedral is considered the house of God. The best-known cathedral of this kind is Milan Cathedral, as well as San Giovanni in Laterano in Rome and those of Alba, Ancona, Mantua, Parma, and Florence's Santa Maria del Fiore. What is this kind of building called in Italy?

Answers to Quiz 5

1. Richard Burton

2. Charlie's Angels

3. Black Ice

4. Pablo Escobar

5. Duomo

Quiz 6

1. Dwayne Johnson is an American actor and former star of the WWE wrestling shows. His grandfather, Peter Maivia and father, Rocky Johnson, were also wrestlers. He has since become an action star, acting in some of the films in the Fast and Furious series, San Andreas, and in HBO TV show Ballers. Back in his wrestling days, his move was called The People's Elbow. What was his name as a wrestler?

2. What major tennis tournament is held annually towards the end of January? Since its inaugural run in 1905, it is the very first Grand Slam competition of the year. It is held at Melbourne Park and features men's and women's singles, men's, women's, and mixed doubles, and junior's championships. This year's champions were Roger Federer and Serena Williams. What is the name of this event?

3. The Rumble in the Jungle was one of the greatest events in the history of boxing and sport itself. It took place in 1974 in what was then Zaire and drew in crowds and other famous people. Muhammad Ali won by knockout, putting his opponent down just before the end of the eighth round. It has been called "arguably the greatest sporting event of the 20th century." Who did Ali fight against?

4. What semiaquatic egg-laying mammal originates from eastern Australia? It is the only mammal that lays eggs, and when it was first discovered in 1799, its body was thought to have been a fake, made of several animals sewn together. Its discovery was thought to be a hoax. What is the name of this animal?

5. What is the largest lake in Europe and the 14th largest freshwater lake by area in the world? It is located in Northwestern Russia. It has an average surface area of 17,891 km2. Its north-to-south length is 219 km, its average width is 83 km, and its average depth is 51 m. Name this lake.

Answers to Quiz 6

1. The Rock

2. Australian Open

3. George Foreman

4. Platypus

5. Lake Ladoga

Quiz 7

1. What is the name of what is probably the most famous fashion magazine in the world? For many years, the American edition was edited by Anna Wintour. It began as a weekly newspaper in 1892 in the United States, and now it is a foremost authority in the fashion world. Its September issues is one of the most important publications of the year. Name this magazine.

2. This is a ballet composed by Tchaikovsky and is now one of the most popular and most performed ballets across the world. The plot follows Odette, a princess turned into a swan by a curse. What's the name of this ballet?

3. What is a traditional French appetizer consisting of sliced or whole raw vegetables which are typically dipped in a vinaigrette or other dipping sauce? They often include celery sticks, carrot sticks, cucumber sticks, bell pepper strips, broccoli, cauliflower, fennel, and asparagus spears, and sometimes olives, depending on local custom. What is the name of this dish?

4. What is the 5th book in the Harry Potter series? The book follows Harry's fifth year at Hogwarts, the return of the Lord Voldemort, and O.W.L. exams. The novel was published on 21 June 2003, and a movie adaptation was released in 2007. What is the name of this book?

5. In religion, what four-letter word is a declaration of affirmation used both in the Hebrew Bible and the New Testament? In modern faith, it is a word that is uttered at the end of a prayer or to convey agreement. What is this word?

Answers to Quiz 7

1. Vogue Magazine

2. Swan Lake

3. Crudite

4. Harry Potter & the Order of the Phoenix

5. Amen

Quiz 8

1. What is a disease resulting from a lack of vitamin C? It affected sailors who went without vitamin C for months, so ships started carrying limes to protect the crew. If you have this disease, you would experience bleeding from the gums and bleeding from the skin. Name this disease.

2. The festive season is special because so many different faiths celebrate special observances. It isn't just Christmas for Christians, it is also Hanukkah for the Jewish. Another celebration is held between December 20 and January 1 to commemorate the African heritage and culture in African-America communities. First observed in the 1960s, it involves feasts, gift-giving, and celebrations. What is this celebration called?

3. This is a mental practice that is centered on achieving a calm state of mind by paying attention to the breath and being grounded in awareness of the present moment. It's also used as a visualization tool, a practice to overcome negativity, or just to promote positive energy and positive thinking. It has many different offshoots, including mindfulness, which is used to help people who suffer from anxiety. It's also used in conjunction with other practices like yoga or prayer. What is this practice called?

4. This American cartoon follows the adventures of a young genius who has a secret laboratory in his parents' home. Screened on Cartoon Network, it also features the boy's sister Dee Dee, his computer, and his nemesis Mandark. Much of the episodes centered on different experiments this boy would carry out or his inventions and his sister's plots to annoy him. What was the name of this cartoon?

5. This is a ceramic material made by heating materials like kaolin, glass, bone, ash, quartz, and alabaster. These materials have to be burnt at temperatures of about 1,200 and 1,400 °C. Its expense comes from its toughness, strength, and translucence. First created in China between

206 BC and 220 AD, it started getting exported about 2000 years ago. Because of where it comes from, this material and the items it creates are called china. It is a very long-lasting material that is very expensive in its antique form. What is the name of this material?

Answers to Quiz 8

1. Scurvy

2. Kwanzaa

3. Meditation

4. Dexter's Laboratory

5. Porcelain

Quiz 9

1. This airline is known as the Royal Dutch carrier, and it was founded in 1919, making it the oldest airline in the world still operating under its original name. It operates scheduled passenger and cargo services to 145 destinations. What is the name of this airline?

2. This sport was dropped as an Olympic event in 1920. It is a test of strength where two teams pull a rope to see who can pull the rope the greater distance and topple the other side first. The sport originates in ancient Egypt, Greece, and China, where it was held in legend that the Sun and Moon played Tug of War over the light and darkness. What is the name of this sport?

3. This is an ancient limestone wall in the Old City of Jerusalem, which is near the foot of the Temple Mount. It is a relatively small segment of the longer Western Wall, and a site where many pilgrims go to pray. It was part of an extension of the Second Jewish Temple which was built by Herod the Great. It's a site that is important for both Christians and Jews. What is the name of this wall?

4. This is a historic and iconic theatre in Moscow, Russia, which holds a lot of prestigious ballets and opera performances. Before the October Revolution, it was a part of the Imperial Theatres of the Russian Empire. This theatre's ballet and opera companies are among the oldest and most renowned in the world. Name this theatre.

5. This American television producer is best known for the Law and Order franchise and a lot of his work in the crime genre on television. He has been very active since 1990, with six police/courtroom dramas and four international spinoffs. He developed Law and Order, one of TVs longest running shows, Law and Order SVU, and Law and Order: Criminal Intent. More recently he created the Chicago franchise, which includes Chicago Fire, Chicago PD, and Chicago Med. What is this man's name?

Answers to Quiz 9

1. KLM
2. Tug of war
3. The Wailing Wall
4. Bolshoi theatre
5. Dick Wolf

Quiz 10

1. A transform fault occurs at a zone where two tectonic plates move against each other in sideways motion. What is the name of the prominent one that exists in California? It extends about 1,200 kilometers through California, and it is where the Pacific Plate meets the North American plate. It is also the name of movie starring Dwayne Johnson. Name this transform fault.

2. Popeye the Sailor is a cartoon character who gets his strength from eating spinach, and his love interest is Olive Oyl. What was the name of his nemesis?

3. This is an open world action-adventure video game series developed by Rockstar Games. The game is set in fictional American cities that are similar to big cities like New York and Miami. In the game, the player has missions that include action-adventure, driving, third-person shooting, and racing elements. Name the video game.

4. Which boxer did Floyd Mayweather fight on May 2, 2015, in what was called The Fight of the Century? Mayweather Jr. beat his opponent by unanimous decision. The fight was highly anticipated but turned out to be a letdown. Who was the opponent in this fight?

5. What was an American teen drama television series about the fictional lives of a close-knit group of friends that ran from 1998 to 2003. The series starred James Van der Beek as Dawson Leery, Katie Holmes, Joshua Jackson, and it was the show that launched Katie Holmes' stardom. Name this show.

Answers to Quiz 10

1. San Andreas fault
2. Bluto or Brutus
3. Grand theft auto
4. Manny Pacquiao
5. Dawson's Creek

Quiz 11

1. What American group consists of rappers will.i.am, apl.de.ap, Taboo, and Fergie? Originally, they were an alternative hip hop group without Fergie. When she joined, they gained more mainstream popularity with songs like *Where is the Love*, *Shut Up* and *Don't Phunk With My Heart*. They eventually adopted a dance-pop style and achieved global success with hits like Imma Be, Rock Your Body, and I Got a Feeling. What is the name of the group?

2. What German passenger airship caught fire in Manchester in the state of New Jersey on May 6, 1937? The disaster claimed the lives of 35 people on board. Before its crash, it was a highly luxurious flight which cut the time of traveling across the Atlantic by ship in half. What was the name of this ill-fated airship?

3. Corsica is a mountainous island located in the Mediterranean Sea. It is located southeast of the French mainland and west of the Italian Peninsula. It was part of the British Empire for a short time in the 18th century, but it was annexed in 1769. The person who invented Coca-Cola was from Corsica. Which country annexed the island from Britain and still owns the island today?

4. Which West African nation's flag consists of 3 vertical stripes which are colored green and white? This consists of 36 states and a Federal Capital Territory. This oil-producing nation's capital is Abuja, and the current leader is Muhammadu Buhari. It is also home to Nollywood, a highly successful and prolific film industry. What is the name of this country?

5. This is a kind of dessert that is made when you whip egg whites, a bit of salt, and sugar until the mixture stiffens. Some recipes can have lemon added to them. If made correctly, the dessert should just melt in your mouth. It can be eaten as is, or can be used as the basis of other desserts. What is the name of this dessert?

Answers to Quiz 11

1. Black Eyed Peas

2. Hindenburg

3. France

4. Nigeria

5. Meringue

Quiz 12

1. This is a type of interaction in the animal kingdom that is known as a win-win. It occurs when there are two animals in the same habitat who get a benefit from living in the same space. It takes place when two organisms benefit from their relationship. Animals with this kind of relationship include sea anemones and hermit crabs, oxpeckers and various larger mammals, as well as ants and fungi. What is this kind of relationship called?

2. This is an American cable and satellite television channel that launched in 1981. It rose to popularity for its celebration of youth culture and playing of music videos of the time. It also gained its foothold with the youth with shows like Total Request Live, Cribs, and Making the Video. The network also has its own award show called the VMAs. Nowadays, it features reality TV shows like Catfish, Ridiculousness, and Teen Mom. What is the name of this channel?

3. This legendary rapper was born in New York and grew up in Compton, California. He was also a talented actor who starred alongside Janet Jackson in Poetic Justice. He has sold over 75 million records worldwide, and his albums All Eyez on Me and his Greatest Hits are among the best-selling albums in the United States. He is one of the most respected and loved rappers, who was known for talking about deeper issues in his music. His greatest songs include Dear Mama, Keep Your Head Up, So Many Tears, and California Love. He still successfully sells records, over 21 years after his death, and in 2017 he was inducted into the Rock and Roll Hall of Fame. What was his name?

4. This man is an American technology and retail entrepreneur, investor, computer scientist, and philanthropist who is best known as the founder, chairman, and CEO of Amazon, as well as one of the wealthiest people in the world. Born in 1964 in New Mexico, he was educated at Princeton University and came up with the idea for Amazon in 1994.

The company is one of the successes that came out of the dot-com bubble of the late 1990s, and it has given this man a net worth of over $8 billion. It is one of the most powerful tech companies in the world. What is the name of the founder of Amazon?

5. This is the second largest city in France and historically a Greek colony. It is one of the most visited cities in Europe and has hosted events like 1998 FIFA World Cup. Landmarks in the city include Notre-Dame de la Garde, the Museum of European and Mediterranean Civilisations, and Château d'If. Its football team primarily wears a blue kit, and its slogan is Droit Au But. What is the name of this city?

Answers to Quiz 12

1. Symbiotic relationship

2. MTV

3. Tupac Shakur

4. Jeff Bezos

5. Marseilles

Quiz 13

1. Which legendary soul singer was blind and used his hard-soled shoes to navigate? He was born in the US State of Georgia, and was named "the Genius of Soul" by Frank Sinatra. He lost his sight young as a result of glaucoma, but that didn't stop him from becoming one of the most successful performers of all time. Hit the Road Jack is one of his most famous hits, and he was portrayed by Jamie Foxx in an Oscar-winning biopic. What was this legends name?

2. Who invented the thermometer and has been called the "father of observational astronomy", the "father of modern physics", and the "father of the scientific method"? Born in Pisa, Italy, he studied speed and velocity, gravity and free fall, the principle of relativity, inertia, and projectile motion. What was this man's name?

3. Which German city endured the worst bombing of World War Two in February 1945? It is situated near the border with the Czech Republic, and it used to house the royal residences for many years. The bombing killed about 25,000 people, and the entire city center was destroyed. It was called the Jewel Box because of its baroque and rococo city centre. Nowadays, it is one of the most visited cities in Germany, with many cultural attractions making it a great place to visit. What is this city's name?

4. In the Muslim faith, the sighting of the new moon signals the start of this religious holiday. Observed worldwide, it celebrates the revelation of the Quran to Muhammad, and it is one of the Five Pillars of Islam. The annual commemoration is characterized by a month-long period of fasting which culminates in celebration through feasting. Name this observance.

5. What island nation produces two-thirds of the world's vanilla? It is located off the coast of East Africa, and over 90% of its wildlife is found nowhere else on Earth. It is also the title of a Dreamworks Animation film that first came out in 2005. What is this island nation's

name?

Answers to Quiz 13

1. Ray Charles

2. Galileo

3. Dresden

4. Ramadan

5. Madagascar

Quiz 14

1. This colorless and odorless liquid is a weapon of mass destruction and a Schedule 1 substance that has been unlawfully used in many conflicts, including the civil war in Syria. It is a man-made nerve agent that was originally designed as a pesticide in 1938. It is dangerous because you can get exposed through skin contact, and symptoms can appear almost immediately after contact. What's this gas called?

2. This former Filipino first lady is known as the "iron butterfly" and is also known for vast collection of shoes and clothing. During her husband's presidency, she amassed a great deal of wealth and lived an incredibly opulent lifestyle. She served as First Lady from 1965 to 1986, and is still one of the richest politicians in the world. Her well-known collection of shoes was even put on display in a museum. What is the name of this woman?

3. The city of Geneva was an independent city state from the Middle Ages until the end of the 18th century. It is home to the headquarters of the United Nations and the seats of dozens of international organizations. Geneva used to be 2 cities. What were their names?

4. The 22nd of November 1963 is one of the most tragic days in history because JFK was assassinated. It was such a big event that it eclipsed the deaths of Aldous Huxley and another famous author. The author is famous for writing a work The Lion, the Witch, and the Wardrobe. Who is this?

5. In architecture, a creepy statue is known as a grotesque. There's another kind of statue that was created with the purpose of channeling rain water so that it doesn't run down masonry walls and erode the mortar between. What is it called?

Answers to Quiz 14

1. Sarin gas

2. Imelda Marcos

3. The Calvinist city of Geneva and the Catholic city of Carrerouge.

4. CS Lewis

5. Gargoyle

Quiz 15

1. In Western cultures, the number 13 is associated with bad luck and as a result some roads don't have a number 13 and some buildings don't have the floor 13. In Japanese culture, there is a similar aversion to a number. The number's pronunciation is similar to the Japanese word for death shi. What is this number?

2. Al Gore is an American politician and environmentalist who served as the 45th Vice President of the United States from 1993 to 2001 under President Bill Clinton. After politics, he became a climate change activist, for which he earned the Nobel Peace Prize in 2007. His documentary, An Inconvenient Truth, won an Academy Award for Best Documentary Feature. Tommy Lee Jones is an American actor best known for roles in Men in Black, Natural Born Killers, and No Country for Old Men. What do these two men have in common?

3. In collective nouns for animals, a group of apes is called a shrewdness, a group of giraffes is called a tower, a group of hyenas is called a cackle, and a group of fish is called a school. A group of ferrets is called a business, a group of leopards is called a leopard, a group of lions is called pride, and a group of elephants is called a parade. What is the collective noun for jellyfish?

4. This northwest Czech city was the last city to be liberated in World War II. It is the 14th largest city in the European Union and the historical capital of Bohemia. One of its monuments is the Dancing House, inspired by Fred Astaire and Ginger Rogers. It is nicknamed the city of 100 spires and is said to have the largest castle in the world. The city is home to about 1.4 million people. What is the name of this city?

5. In the Bible what was called an adamant? Scientifically, it is a metastable allotrope of carbon, where the carbon atoms are arranged in a variation of the face-centered cubic crystal structure. In society, it is a very precious stone that is highly sought after and the material used for many pieces of jewelry including engagement rings and necklaces. It is strong enough to break glass. What is this substance?

Answers to Quiz 15

1. 4

2. They were college roommates.

3. A smack

4. Prague

5. Diamond

Quiz 16

1. Van Halen is one of the most famous hard rock bands of the 20th century. The band went through various name changes and released their first studio album in 1978. They rose to popularity, but the group also went through various line-up changes. Their 7th album, released in 1986, was the very first one without David Lee Roth. For this album and 3 others, their new lead singer was Sammy Hagar, and the album was named after Eddie Van Halen's home studio. The name of the album is also the name of a law in California that allows medical professionals or police to hold someone involuntarily if they are thought to be a danger to themselves and others. What is the name of this album?

2. The Strait of Gibraltar is located between Southern Spain and the North West of Africa. It is known by many names, including the Gate of the West, Al-Zuqaq, "The Passage", Fretum Gatitanum, and even as the "Pillars of Hercules". What sea does it connect the Atlantic Ocean with?

3. Poet Samuel Taylor Coleridge was a prominent member of a group of poets and writers known as The Romantics. He is famous for writing poems like Kubla Khan and Christabel. He was also well-known for his drug use, and he used to disappear on crazy drug binges. He even says Kubla Khan was conceived during these drug binges. What was his drug of choice?

4. This bay is based in California, and it is the home of the famous Golden Gate Bridge. The bay drains 40% of the water that comes out of California. It also housed the almost escape-proof prison that was also known as The Rock. What is the name of this bay?

5. What texts were discovered at Qumran? These famous texts were discovered in 11 caves between 1947 and 1956. They are said to have "great historical, religious, and linguistic significance." The texts are both biblical and non-biblical, and most of them are written in Hebrew, with some written in Aramaic and even Greek. What is the name of these texts?

Answers to Quiz 16

1. 5150

2. Mediterranean

3. Opium

4. San Francisco Bay

5. The Dead Sea Scrolls

Quiz 17

1. This South American country shares borders with Panama, Venezuela, Brazil, Ecuador, and Peru. Its flag is made up of 3 lines that are gold, blue, and red. Its capital city is Bogota, and other notable cities are Cartagena and Medellin. The country is the setting for popular Netflix show, Narcos. What is the name of this country?

2. Radiohead is an English alternative band with the members Thom Yorke, Jonny Greenwood, Colin Greenwood, Ed O'Brien, and Phil Selway. They first rose to fame with their debit single Creep. Some of their most popular albums include Pablo Honey, Kid A, In Rainbows, and The Bends. Their 1997 album has been cited by musicians as one of the greatest albums of all time. It was their third studio album which was self-produced with Nigel Godrich. It includes songs like Paranoid Android, Lucky, and Climbing Up the Walls. What is the name of this album?

3. A Griffin is a mythical creature that is a cross between a lion and a what? It was thought of as king of all creatures and a guardian of treasure and priceless possessions. What bird makes up the other part of a griffin?

4. This is one of the world's oldest known infectious diseases, and it is also known as Hansen's Disease. It is a long-term infection which sees sufferers facing stigma and often exclusion from society. It is even mentioned in the Bible with Jesus healing a man who suffers from it. It is known for heavy disfiguring sores on the skin and nerve damage. Contrary to popular belief, it is not contagious and can be treated. What is the name of this disease?

5. This well-known holiday destination is located between Marseille and La Spezia. Known as the Côte d'Azur, it extends from the Italian border in the east to Saint-Tropez, Hyères, Toulon, or Cassis in the west. Originally, it was as a resort for the British upper class, then it evolved into a holiday destination for aristocrats from other countries. Today, it

hosts many famous people and celebrities, and it is associated with glamour and lavish living. It is also the location of the Cannes Film Festival which hosts many of the rich and famous during the summer. What is the name of this destination?

Answers to Quiz 17

1. Colombia

2. OK Computer

3. Eagle

4. Leprosy

5. The Riviera

Quiz 18

1. This Canadian city is the capital of Manitoba. It is also the largest city of the province. Its name means "muddy water," and historically, it was a trading center for aboriginal peoples. Today, it is known as the "Gateway to the West," and is a railway and transportation hub with a diversified economy. What is the name of this city?

2. This a process of displaying text on a television, video screen, or other visual display to provide additional or interpretive information. It is used as a transcription of the audio portion of a program as it occurs, sometimes including descriptions of non-speech elements. If you go on a YouTube video, it is symbolized by the letters CC below the video. What is the name of this type of transcription?

3. This legendary band was formed in London during the 1960s by students. They were mainly active between 1965 and 1995, and during that time, they achieved global success and fame, and were known as musical pioneers in the alternative rock genre. During their early days, they performed under names including Tea Set, Sigma 6, The Scream-ing Abdabs, and Leonard's Lodgers. They were famous for the use of "philosophical lyrics, sonic experimentation, extended compositions, and elaborate live shows." Group members were Syd Barrett on guitar and lead vocals, Nick Mason on drums, Roger Waters on bass and vocals, and Richard Wright on keyboards and vocals. The Dark Side of the Moon and The Wall became two of their best-selling albums of all time. What is the name of this band?

4. Pufferfish is a dish prepared from the poisonous fish. It is well known as a delicacy favored by the rich, but it is also known for how dangerous it can be to eat if it isn't prepared properly. To make it safe to consume, it must be carefully prepared to remove toxic parts and to avoid contaminating the meat. The restaurant preparation of this fish is strictly controlled by law in Japan and several other countries. What is the Japanese name for the pufferfish?

5. Crackers are made from mixing flour and water. They are considered healthy, nutritious, and are usually eaten as snacks with cheese. They originate from Boston Massachusetts in the late 18th century, where they were given names like sea biscuit. They were eventually given the name cracker because of the sound they made when they burned. Why do crackers have small holes on them?

Answers to Quiz 18

1. Winnipeg

2. Closed Captions

3. Pink Floyd

4. Fugu

5. To prevent air bubbles from ruining the baking process

Quiz 19

1. Jarvis is a highly advanced computerized A.I. we see in the Iron Man and Avengers movies. It is used to manage Tony Stark's life and is his best friend. Based on the Stark family butler, it is voiced by actor Paul Bettany. What does J.A.R.V.I.S. stand for?

2. In cocktails, this drink consists of vodka and tomato juice primarily. It is a common "Hair of the Dog" drink used to cure hangovers. The origin of its name is disputed. Some say it was after Queen Mary I of England. Others think the inspiration for the name was Hollywood star Mary Pickford, while other historians believe it was named after a Chicago waitress called Mary who happened to work in a bar called the Bucket of Blood. What is the name of this cocktail?

3. Barrier reefs are underwater ecosystems that are sometimes called Rainforests of the Sea. They are formed by the secretions of calcium carbonate structures, and the most famous ones are found in Australia and in Belize. They attract many tourists, scientists, divers, and underwater photographers. What are barrier reefs made of?

4. Who wrote the wildly successful play Hamilton and starred as the eponymous character in the Broadway musical. He is an American composer, lyricist, playwright, and actor of Puerto Rican descent. He also wrote the Broadway musical In the Heights. He was won a Pulitzer Prize, two Grammy Awards, an Emmy Award, a MacArthur Fellowship, and three Tony Awards for his notable work on Hamilton. What is this man's name?

5. In September 2017, Apple announced the release of its latest line of iPhones, the iPhone 8 and X. The iPhone revolutionized smartphones and changed the game for users. It also originated many great applications and systems and put the Apple brand into direct competition with Japanese electronics giant Samsung. The phones are now famous for having Siri, a voice assistant, and most recently facial identification. With each new edition, Apple has added new features and led with the

need to make things more convenient for users. They even tried releasing a lower cost version, the 5C. What year was the very first generation of iPhones released?

Answers to Quiz 19

1. Just A Rather Very Intelligent System

2. Bloody Mary

3. Coral

4. Lin Manuel Miranda

5. 2007

Quiz 20

1. This is a landlocked unitary sovereign state in East Asia found between China and Russia. It is the 18th largest country in the world by land mass. The country is known for having very little arable land. Ulaanbaatar, the capital and largest city, is home to less than half of the country's population. What is the name of this country?

2. This is a form of martial arts that brings together dance, fighting, and acrobatics. Developed by African slaves living in Brazil more than 500 years ago, this style of fighting is known for its rhythmic elements and its ability to look like a performance. You can see this style of martial arts on movies like Only the Strong, Bloodsport 2, and Tekken. What's the name of the martial art?

3. This ancient Chinese system's name in English translates to "wind-water" and is used to arrange rooms and furniture to create the best flow of energy. It has been practiced for over 3000 years, but still remains highly trendy in interior decor circles. It's based on the understanding that there is energy flowing around us, and this practice helps people harness the most positive form of energy. What is this practice called?

4. This was a WWII battle fought on 6 June 1944. Also known as D-Day, it was the biggest attack in military history to use air, land, and ocean assaults. It involved as many as 160,000 soldiers. The battle was forged by the Allied powers to defeat the German forces in Western Europe. The battle was also called Operation Overlord and Operation Neptune for the ocean offensive. It was the beginning of the second front of fighting against Germany and was a very big victory for the Allies. What was this battle called?

5. What American television series that premiered in April 2017 is based on a 1985 novel by Canadian writer Margaret Atwood? It stars Elisabeth Moss, Joseph Fiennes, Yvonne Strahovski, and Alexis Bledel, and won Emmy Awards in 2017. The story depicts a future where the

world has fallen into a state where fertility rates collapse, and a totalitarian government takes over to rule the population. This government, the "Gilead," takes over after a Civil War. In this state, women are suppressed and have no rights. What is name of this TV show and book?

Answers to Quiz 20

1. Mongolia

2. Capoeira

3. Feng shui

4. Battle of Normandy

5. The Handmaid's Tale

Quiz 21

1. This wading bird's name is derived from Portuguese or Spanish for "flame-colored". It's usually pink or red in color and is known for standing on one leg while the other is tucked beneath its body. They are found in many parts of the world, and the young of this bird are usually reddish-grey in color and are even sometimes nicknamed as miracle birds. It's not known why they stand on one leg, and many theories have been brought forward. What's the name of this bird?

2. This American rock band was formed in Seattle, Washington, in 1994. It was founded by Nirvana drummer Dave Grohl as a one-man project following the dissolution of Nirvana. The group's name comes from the UFOs and various aerial phenomena that were reported by Allied aircraft pilots in World War II. What is the name of this rock band?

3. What travel destination is the setting for the pray portion of Eat, Pray, Love? It is made up of three islands: Nusa Penida, Nusa Lembongan, and Nusa Ceningan. It is located between Java and Lombok to the east, and its capital is called Denpasar. It is a world-famous travel destination, and tourism-related business makes up 80% of its economy. It has a very high density of spas, and it is reported this is where David Bowie's ashes are scattered. What is this place called?

4. What is the official name for a type of bicycle that had a large front wheel and a much smaller rear wheel? It was popular in the 19th century in Europe and across the Atlantic in the United States. Because of the difference in size of the two wheels, a lot of riders got injured trying to get off it. Name this kind off bicycle.

5. Who was the eighth and last president of the Soviet Union? He was the country's head of state from 1988 until 1991, when the Union was dissolved. What was his name?

Answers to Quiz 21

1. Flamingo

2. Foo Fighters

3. Bali

4. Penny farthing

5. Mikhail Gorbachev

Quiz 22

1. Antarctica is one of two continents that has never been the site of a military conflict. What's the other one? This continent is home to Uluru or Ayers Rock, Sydney Opera House, and The Great Barrier reef. Originally, the place was a penal continent, and today it is one of the most developed and vibrant countries that hosts sporting events and other cultural attractions. What is this continent?

2. What is the name of the love song performed by American rock band Aerosmith? It is on the soundtrack for the 1998 film Armageddon which starred Bruce Willis. This song was Aerosmith's biggest hit, debuting at number 1 on the U.S. Billboard Hot 100. It has the lyrics, "I don't want to close my eyes, I don't want to fall asleep, coz I'd miss you baby." Name this song.

3. Cuba is a country that is rich in culture and tradition with influences pulled from Africa, Europe, and indigenous American influences. The Cuban people eat dishes mainly based on rice, beans, and meat. Their coffee is well-known and loved across the world, and the country's culture is also synonymous with the production of high quality cigars. People in Cuba also drink rum and another well-known alcoholic cocktail that is filled with mint leaves. What is the name of this cocktail?

4. In April 1986, a flawed nuclear reactor located in what is now Ukraine in the Soviet Union exploded. It is probably one of the biggest nuclear accidents to take place in history, and its effects were far reaching and can still be seen in Pripyat, the city where it took place. Two people died directly in the accident, and 28 others lost their lives as a result of radiation poisoning. People near the area had to be resettled to escape the radiation. The accident was caused by a flawed reactor and technician error. What was the name of this event?

5. In baking, what is the name of a traditionally red, red-brown, or "mahogany" colored cake layered with white cream cheese icing?

Answers to Quiz 22

1. Australia

2. I Don't Want to Miss a Thing

3. Mojito

4. Chernobyl disaster

5. Red velvet cake

Quiz 23

1. She was a Dutch exotic dancer and courtesan who was a spy in the First World War. She got her status as a spy because of her ability to cross international borders freely since the Netherlands remained neutral. She travelled between France and the Netherlands and ultimately attracted attention. What was her name?

2. This Southeast Asian country was formerly known as Siam. It is a heavily travelled tourist destination which attracts people because of great beaches and nightlife. The nation's capital is Bangkok, and popular places people visit include Chiang Mai and Ko Samui. The country is home to around 66 million people, and it is bordered by Myanmar, Laos, Malaysia, and Cambodia. What is the name of this country?

3. This is a horticultural practice in which people remove the diseased, damaged, dead, non-productive parts of a plant. It is instrumental in the regrowth of healthy plant tissue, and is a practice commonly applied to roses. What is the name of this process?

4. This was the first independent credit card company in the world, which was established as an independent company for travelers and entertainment. It was founded in 1950, and operates in 59 countries around the world. Name this credit card.

5. The strelitzia is a plant that originates in South Africa. It is named after the birthplace of Queen Charlotte of the United Kingdom. In South Africa, it is commonly known as a crane flower and is featured on the reverse of the 50-cent coin. It is the floral emblem of the City of Los Angeles. What is a common name used for the flower based the animal it resembles?

Answers to Quiz 23

1. Mata Hari

2. Thailand

3. Pruning

4. Diners Club International

5. Bird of paradise

Quiz 24

1. What is lygophobia the fear of? It's a common fear children have, and the origin of the word is actually the Greek word for shadow. This fear can arise from different factors and forces, including traumatic events or predispositions. What is lygophobia the fear of?

2. In weather, a thermometer is used to measure temperature, a hygrometer measures humidity, an anemometer is used for measuring wind speed, a pyranometer is used for measuring solar radiation, and a rain gauge measures liquid precipitation. What is the name of a scientific instrument used to measure atmospheric pressure?

3. Rhinoplasty is a plastic surgery procedure for correcting and reconstructing the form, restoring the functions, aesthetically enhancing a part of the body, and resolving trauma or congenital defect. What body part is this procedure performed on?

4. This was a critically acclaimed science fiction film that was released in 2010, directed by Christopher Nolan. The film stars Leonardo DiCaprio as a professional thief who steals information by infiltrating the subconscious. As a final job he takes in exchange for his freedom, he has to implant an idea into a wealthy businessman's subconscious. He assembles a team that can help him do it so he can get back to his two children. The stellar cast includes Ken Watanabe, Joseph Gordon-Levitt, Marion Cotillard, Tom Hardy, Cillian Murphy, and Michael Caine. What is the name of this film?

5. This a twin island country located off the northern coast of South American mainland. Historically, it was a Spanish colony, but it has also been a part of the British, French, and Dutch empires. One of this nation's most popular tourist attractions is the Carnival, and it's also home to a rich musical culture. It has a red flag with a black line diagonally going from top left to bottom right. Name this country.

Answers to Quiz 24

1. Darkness

2. Barometer

3. Nose

4. Inception

5. Trinidad and Tobago

Quiz 25

1. She is an English supermodel and actress who started working at age of 15 modeling for some of the greatest designers and brands. She was very famous in the 1990s as part of a group of the most famous and sought-after models in the world. She also appeared in music videos for Michael Jackson and George Michael, to name a few. She is of Jamaican descent and recently launched an acting career, appearing in shows like Empire. She has also been the subject of a scandal in which she was accused of hitting her assistant with a cellphone. What is this supermodel's name?

2. Bob Marley is arguably one of the most important musicians and public figures of the 20th century. He made some of the most famous songs that we still listen to and celebrate today. In his performing days, he had a band that provided vocals and instrumental support. The band included Junior Braithwaite, Peter Tosh, Neville Livingston, and Cherry Smith. What was the name of this band?

3. This legendary crooner was known as Napoleon to the secret service, and he was also commonly nicknamed Ol' Blue Eyes. He is one of the best-selling music artists of all time, having sold more than 150 million records worldwide. Born in Hoboken, New Jersey, to Italian immigrants, he began his musical career in the swing era. A lot of his songs are classics and standards performed and covered by other musicians. Some of his most successful songs include *The Way You Look Tonight, My Way, I've Got You Under My Skin, Love and Marriage, Strangers in the Night*, and *New York, New York*. He died in 1998 at the age of 82. His daughter Nancy also had a singing career. What is this legend's name?

4. In Greek myths, she was considered the most beautiful woman in the world. She was at the center of the Trojan War when she fell in love and eloped with Prince Paris of Troy. She was played by Diane Kruger in the 2004 film Troy. What was this woman's name?

5. This is Swiss luxury watchmaker and one of the most powerful brands in the world. The name of the brand was thought to sound like a watch being wound. The brand also sponsors a number of events in tennis, motorsport, and golf. Tiger Woods used to be an endorser of this brand. Name this watch brand.

Answers to Quiz 25

1. Naomi Campbell

2. The Wailers

3. Frank Sinatra

4. Helen of Troy

5. Rolex

Quiz 26

1. This saint is considered a heroine of France for her role during the Lancastrian phase of the Hundred Years' War and was canonized as a Roman Catholic saint. She said she received visions of the Archangel Michael, Saint Margaret, and Saint Catherine of Alexandria instructing her to support Charles VII and recover France from English domination late in the Hundred Years' War. What was her name?

2. This is a small island nation that also happens to be the largest economy that isn't in the UN. It is one of the biggest economies in the world, with a world-renowned high-tech industry, and is highly ranked in terms of freedom of the press, healthcare, public education, economic freedom, and human development. Its capital city is Taipei, and it has been independent since 1950, but it is considered a rebel nation by China. It is one of Asia's biggest traders and it has a population of over 23 million. What is the name of this country?

3. Sherlock Holmes is a private detective who was made popular in the late 19th century and was written by Arthur Conan Doyle. He was a very intelligent man who solved crimes for clients and used his deductive reasoning ability to extrapolate information commonly missed by other people, even the police. He was a very popular character back when the books first came out, and even today he is a popular character who has spun TV shows like NBC's Elementary, BBCs Sherlock, and the Sherlock Holmes movies starring Robert Downey Jr. The stories feature Sherlock's companion and friend Dr. Watson who writes most of the stories. Some of the stories also feature his brother. What was Sherlock Holmes' brother's name?

4. The Northern Lights are collisions between electrically charged particles from the sun that enter the earth's atmosphere. The lights are seen above the magnetic poles of the northern and southern hemispheres, and are also called auroras. They give the sky a beautiful yellow-green color and are such a great thing to see that people travel to

see them. Name a country you would see the lights in.

5. Which country had a commercial, economic, and financial embargo imposed on it by the United States? The political action is also known el bloqueo, that was put in place in the late 1950s, during the Fulgencio Batista regime. What nation experienced this embargo?

Answers to Quiz 26

1. Joan of Arc

2. Taiwan

3. Mycroft Holmes

4. Scotland, Norway, Iceland, Finland, Sweden, Canada

5. Cuba

Quiz 27

1. This is legendary pop group hails from Sweden and is one of the most successful acts of the disco era. The group famously won the Eurovision Song Contest in 1974, and was made of the members Agnetha Fältskog, Björn Ulvaeus, Benny Andersson, and Anni-Frid Lyngstad. They sold between140 to over 500 million sold records across the world and had many hits including Gimme, Gimme, Gimme, Waterloo, as well as Money, Money, Money. What is the name of this band?

2. Tasseography is a divination or fortune-telling method that interprets patterns in the leaves of which beverage? The term derives from the French word for cup. The reading is used to learn about a person's life events, and it is one of the practices carried out by fortune tellers. What leaves are read in tasseography?

3. The Die Hard series follows the adventures of John McClane, a New York City and Los Angeles police detective who continually finds himself in the middle of crises where he is able to stop the bad guys and save the day. It was one of the most successful movie franchises of the 1980s and 1990s and raised Bruce Willis' profile. Which failed script of a sequel starring Arnold Schwarzenegger was it originated from?

4. Where on your body is your patella located? According to Wikipedia, "it is a small, freestanding, bone that rests between the femur (thighbone) and tibia (shinbone)". Injury of the patella results in difficulty walking, running, standing, or engaging in athletic activity. Where on your body do you find the patella?

5. This important historic artifact was discovered in 1799 by one of Napoleon's soldiers. It is an inscribed stone that weights about 1 tonne. Written on it is a royal decree from Memphis in the Egyptian empire. The decree is written in three languages, hieroglyphics, Egyptian demotic, and Greek. It took experts over 20 years to decipher all the inscriptions. It used to be a much larger stone that broke apart over

time. It is now on display at London's British Museum where it has been kept since 1802. The name of this stone is also the name of a language software. What is the name of this stone?

Answers to Quiz 27

1. ABBA

2. Tea

3. Commando

4. Knee

5. The Rosetta Stone

Quiz 28

1. Which organ in the human body has a name that translates as "all flesh?" Part of it is sandwiched between the stomach and the spine. The other part is nestled in the curve of the duodenum (first part of the small intestine).

2. Which middle name did UK Prime Minister Winston Churchill share with Charlie Chaplin? It's also the name of Criminal Minds character, Dr. Reid.

3. In the original story of Cinderella, one of the evil stepsisters cut off her toes to fit into the glass slippers. What gruesome end did the sisters meet after Cinderella is found to be the true owner of the slippers?

4. A jiffy is an actual unit of time, not just an expression. In computer engineering, it is the length of one cycle of the computer's system clock. What is a jiffy in chemistry and physics?

5. Who wrote that the female of the species is deadlier that the male? His works of fiction include The Jungle Book, and he is considered to be a major innovator in the art of the short story. His children's books are classics of children's literature, and one critic described his work as exhibiting "a versatile and luminous narrative gift." What was his name?

Answers to Quiz 28

1. Pancreas

2. Spencer

3. Their eyes were pecked out by birds

4. A jiffy is the amount of time it takes light to travel a distance of one centimeter

5. Rudyard Kipling

Quiz 29

1. Which boys name means "he who resembles God"? This is the name of the King of Pop, one of the greatest basketball players of all time, and Catherine Zeta Jones' husband.

2. Madonna has had top 10 singles like Borderline, Like a Virgin, and Into the Groove. What was her first? It was her breakout track which features the lyrics, "You can turn this world around, and bring back all of those happy days. Put your troubles down." Name this song.

3. What is a form of traditional mining that extracts gold from a placer deposit using a pan? The process is one of the simplest ways to extract gold. In many parts of the world it was abandoned because it leads to major soil erosion and damage to the environment. What is it called?

4. What is the practice of advancing clocks during summer months so that evening daylight lasts longer? This usually happens at the start of the spring, and only an adjustment of 1 hour is made to clocks. What is the name of this process?

5. This is an Italian luxury vehicle manufacturer established in 1914 in Bologna. Its tagline is "Luxury, sports, and style cast in exclusive cars," and the brand's mission statement is to "build ultra-luxury performance automobiles with timeless Italian style, accommodating bespoke interiors, and effortless, signature-sounding power". The company's headquarters are now in Modena, and its emblem is a trident. What is the name of this car maker?

Answers to Quiz 29

1. Michael

2. Holiday

3. Gold panning

4. Daylight saving time

5. Maserati

Quiz 30

1. In emergency situations, this process is used to determine which injured people should receive medical attention first, based on how serious and how treatable they are. This especially happens out in the field. The term comes from the French meaning to separate, sift, or select. What is the name of this process?

2. This man was a famous businessman, investor, pilot, and film industry genius who was incredibly wealthy, becoming a millionaire at age 18. He was also incredibly troubled with OCD and pain from injuries he got in a plane crash. He was born in 1905 and died in 1976, at which point he had become a major recluse. He famously dated Katherine Hepburn and broke a world record for a flight around the world. His famous plane was known as the Spruce Goose. He was the subject of the movie The Aviator, where he was portrayed by Leonardo Di-Caprio. What is his name?

3. The Mustang was originally unveiled in 1964, and is a classic American muscle car. It appeared in many famous films, including Goldfinger. It was created to compete with the Chevrolet Camaro, Pontiac Firebird, AMC Javelin, Chrysler Plymouth Barracuda, and the Dodge Challenger. Which car manufacturer created the Mustang?

4. This Italian city is the capital of Campania and the third-largest municipality after Rome and Milan. It is the 9th most populous urban area in the European Union, and it is well-known for landmarks like Teatro di San Carlo, Mount Vesuvius, Piazza del Plebiscito, and Castel Nuovo. Diego Maradona once played for this city's football team. What is this city's name?

5. This British rock band was born in Birmingham in the 1960s, and is made up of the members Tony Iommi, bassist and main lyricist Geezer Butler, singer Ozzy Osbourne, and drummer Bill Ward. They are heavy metal originators and one of the great bands of the 1970s. They have sold over 70 million records, and they were inducted into the Hall of

Fame in 2006. Their biggest tracks include Paranoid and Iron Man. What is the name of this band?

Answers to Quiz 30

1. Triage

2. Howard Hughes

3. Ford

4. Naples

5. Black Sabbath

Quiz 31

This type of poem originated from Italy and became a form that was studied across the world, even today. The poem structure is fourteen lines following a strict rhyme scheme and specific structure. According to Wikipedia, "Guittone d'Arezzo brought it to Tuscany where he adapted it to his language when he founded the Siculo-Tuscan School, or Guittonian School of Poetry." The poem is made up of 14 lines, which are divided into smaller sections also known as quatrains. The rhyme structure of this kind of poem is strict. There is even a Shakespearean version of this poem, which follows the rhyming structure of ABAB / CDCD / EFEF / GG. They are written in what is known as an iambic pentameter. What is the name of this kind of poem?

2. What is the paneling that is attached to the back of a stovetop or to the wall behind a kitchen countertop to protect against splashed liquids?

3. The Spanish steps are a monumental stairway of 135 steps built with French diplomat Étienne Gueffier's bequeathed funds of 20,000 scudi, in 1723–1725, linking the Bourbon Spanish Embassy and the Trinità dei Monti church. In which city are they found?

4. The International Criminal Court is an intergovernmental organization and international tribunal that sits in the Netherlands. It has the power of try individuals for international war crimes and crimes against humanity. In what city is this court located?

5. On Game of Thrones, the House Lannister of Casterly Rock is one of the Great Houses of Westeros. It is also the current house that rules the Seven Kingdoms. The most prominent members of this family are Cersei and Jaime, the former who is currently the queen sitting on the Iron Throne. The Lannisters come from Casterly Rock, but as the ruling family currently live in King's Landing. Their flag is red and gold and has the symbol of a lion, and their official motto is "Hear Me Roar." What is their unofficial slogan?

Answers to Quiz 31

1. Sonnet

2. Backsplash

3. Rome

4. The Hague

5. A Lannister always pays their debt

Quiz 32

1. This is a bladed weapon that was designed to fit underneath a gun like a rifle. Originating in 17th century France, it was used in close-quarters combat. It was largely phased out because it was found to only be responsible for 1% of deaths on the battlefield, so it became obsolete. What is the name of this weapon?

2. He is a Canadian rapper, singer, actor, and entrepreneur whose first name is Aubrey. He first became known for acting in the show Degrassi, and then he rose to fame releasing rap mixtapes and singles. He was signed to Young Money Entertainment and released his first studio album, Thank Me Later, in 2010, which had hits like Miss Me, Over, and Fireworks. He has since released albums that include Views and Take Care, and one of his most popular songs is Hotline Bling. What is the name of this rapper?

3. Matthew the Apostle was, according to the Christian Bible, one of the twelve apostles of Jesus and, according to Christian tradition, one of the four Evangelists. What was his occupation before becoming a disciple?

4. This was a French artist and Impressionist painter, known for both his use of colour and his fluid and original draughtsmanship. His early works displayed the Fauvism style. He is commonly regarded, along with Pablo Picasso, as one of the artists who defined the great leaps in visual art that ushered in the movements of the early 20th century. His famous paintings include Blue Nude, Woman with a Hat, and Green Stripe. Name this artist.

5. This was a 20th century art movement under the greater movement of Impressionism. It was originated from the three-dimensional works created by Paul Cézanne, but the artists that brought it to prominence are Georges Braque and Pablo Picasso. Most of Picasso's famous works are within this movement. Images are represented as angular and three-dimensional, and this style is even applied to people. What is the name of this movement?

Answers to Quiz 32

1. Bayonet

2. Drake

3. Tax collector

4. Henri Matisse

5. Cubism

Quiz 33

1. Dante Alighieri was a famous poet born in Florence, Italy, in the 13th century. He is considered one of the most important poets of the Middle Ages, and his famous epic The Divine Comedy is considered one of the best Italian works of all time. His work The Inferno tells the journey of the poet's journey through hell with the poet Virgil. According to Wikipedia, "Hell is depicted as nine concentric circles of torment located within the Earth." It shows what becomes of the people who abandon virtues in favor of sins and fleshly desires. It represents the journey of the soul toward. What is the fifth circle of hell?

2. This state is located in the north coast of Borneo. It is surrounded by the state of Sarawak. The state used to be a lot bigger and was part of a greater empire ruled by Sultan Bolkiah from 1485 to 1528. It's a wealthy state, boasting one of the highest standards of living in the world. The state was a British protectorate since 1888, and it gained independence in 1984. What is the name of this state?

3. The Arab Kingdom of Jordan is located in Western Asia. It is bordered by Saudi Arabia, Iraq, Syria, Israel, Palestine, and the Dead Sea. The country's capital is Amman, and it came into existence after WWI. Who is the king and head of state of Jordan?

4. This female garment from India consists of a crop top and skirt that is worn inside of a long drape of fabric that is typically wrapped around the waist, with one end draped over the shoulder, baring the midriff. It can be worn daily, and fancier more elaborate versions are worn at special occasions like weddings. What is the name of this garment?

5. The Sound of Music is a 1965 musical film starring Julie Andrews and Christopher Plummer. The film is an adaptation of the 1959 Broadway musical of the same name, composed by Richard Rodgers with lyrics by Oscar Hammerstein II. Based on the memoir, The Story of the Trapp Family Singers, by Maria von Trapp, the film is about a young Austrian woman studying to become a nun in Salzburg in 1938

who is sent to the villa of a retired naval officer and widower to be governess to his seven children. In which country did The Sound of Music take place?

Answers to Quiz 33

1. Wrath

2. Brunei

3. King Abdullah

4. Sari

5. Austria

Quiz 34

1. She is an American singer, songwriter, actress, and next to Britney Spears, one of the most famous female pop stars of the early 2000s. She was a member of The Mickey Mouse Club when she was younger and rose to fame with songs like Genie in a Bottle. She has also acted in movies like Burlesque and is a mentor on the musical competition The Voice. What is her name?

2. Marble is a metamorphic rock composed of recrystallized carbonate minerals, most commonly calcite or dolomite. Marble may be foliated. Marble is commonly used for sculpture and as a building material. Marble is formed by the metamorphosis of which rock?

3. What punctuation mark separates major sentence elements? It can be used between two closely related independent clauses. They can also be used in place of commas to separate items in a list, particularly when the elements of that list contain commas. What is this punctuation mark?

4. This is a 3D computer film produced by Pixar Animation Studios for Walt Disney Pictures. Released on 5 June 2013, it is a prequel to 2001's Monsters, Inc. It tells the story of two monsters, studying to become master monsters at university. They start off as rivals but slowly become best friends who realize how good they are working as a team. Voices of the characters include John Goodman, Billy Crystal, Steve Buscemi, and Bob Peterson. What is this movie's name?

Which Star Wars character was introduced in the 2015 film, Star Wars: The Force Awakens, and is portrayed by Adam Driver? The character is the son of Han Solo and Leia Organa, and is Darth Vader's grandson, but he has moved over to the dark side under the Supreme Leader Snoke. What is this character's name?

Answers to Quiz 34

1. Christina Aguilera

2. Limestone

3. Semicolon

4. Monsters University

5. Kylo Ren

Quiz 35

1. Rain forests are characterized by high rainfall, with annual rainfall in the case of tropical rainforests between 250 and 450 cm (98 and 177 in), and definitions varying by region for temperate rainforests. The biggest rainforest is the Amazon, which covers a great part of the North East of South America. In which area of the world do tropical rainforests occur?

2. Michael Jackson began his solo career in 1979 with Off the Wall, which sold over 25 million albums worldwide. Next, he released the wildly successful Thriller in 1982. He followed this with Bad in 1987 and Dangerous in 1991. What is the name of the album he released on June 18, 1995? It was his fifth album released through Epic Records. It consists of two discs, and its songs include *"You Are Not Alone", "Earth Song", "This Time Around", "They Don't Care About Us"*, and *"Stranger in Moscow"*. Name this album.

3. Astraphobia is the fear of thunder or lightning, heliophobia is the fear of the sun, and deipnophobia is the fear of dinner parties. Allodoxaphobia is the fear of opinions, coulrophobia is the fear of clowns, genuphobia is the fear of knees, and agoraphobia is a fear of open spaces. If you have triskaidekaphobia what are you afraid of?

4. The NBA is made up of 30 teams, and this team is based in Los Angeles, California. It is part of the Western Conference Pacific division and wears purple and gold. This team is one of the richest and most successful teams in the league which has had some important players, including Kobe Bryant. They play their games at Staples Centers and have 16 championships to their name. What is the name of this team?

5. What is Italian ice cream called? It comes from the word for frozen and it is made with a base of milk, cream, and sugar, and is flavored with fruit and nut purees. According to Wikipedia, "it is generally lower in fat but higher in sugar than other styles of ice cream. It typically con-

tains less air and more flavoring than other kinds of frozen desserts, giving it a density and richness that distinguishes it from other ice creams." Name this ice cream.

Answers to Quiz 35

1. On or near the equator

2. HIStory

3. The number 13

4. LA Lakers

5. Gelato

Quiz 36

1. Twilight is a four-part set of books in the fantasy romance genre. It was very popular between 2005 and 2008. The story follows the love story of a teenage girl, Bella, and a vampire called Edward Cullen. Who wrote the Twilight series?

2. This is a phrase that describes serial literature produced during the nineteenth century in the United Kingdom. It refers to cheap literature that was sold each week which cost a penny. Most of the stories were focused on detectives, criminals, or supernatural entities. It is also the name of a British-American horror drama television series starring Eva Green. What is this term?

3. Who was the 5th prime minister of Israel who ruled between 1992 and 1995? He served two terms and was then assassinated on 4 November 1995 in Tel Aviv. What was this politician's name?

4. This is a group of traditionalist Christian church fellowships with Swiss Anabaptist origins. They are known for simple living, plain dress, and reluctance to adopt many conveniences of modern technology. The history of the church began with a schism in Switzerland within a group of Swiss and Alsatian Anabaptists in 1693 led by Jakob Ammann. What is the name of this church and its people?

5. This event takes place either when the Moon passes between the Sun and Earth, or when the Moon blocks the Sun. This can happen only at new moon when the Sun and the Moon are in conjunction. The three types of this event are, total, partial, and annular. The Western hemisphere experienced one in September 2017. What is the name of this phenomena?

Answers to Quiz 36

1. Stephanie Meyer

2. Penny dreadful

3. Yitzhak Rabin

4. Amish

5. Solar eclipse

Quiz 37

1. This is an Italian football team that hails from Turin, Piedmont. The team famously wears a black and white vertical striped kit and is nicknamed Vecchia Signora or "The Old Lady". The club is one of the most successful teams in Europe with thirty-three official league titles, twelve Coppa Italia titles, and seven national Super Cups titles, two Intercontinental Cups, two European Champion Clubs' Cup and UEFA Champions Leagues, one European Cup Winners' Cup, a national record of three UEFA Cups, two UEFA Super Cups, and one UEFA Intertoto Cup. What is the name of this team?

2. This is an American actor, producer, and director, best known for her role as Monica Geller on Friends. She was once featured in a Bruce Springsteen video, and she also owns her own successful production company and was married to actor David Arquette. What is the name of this actress?

3. This term comes from a Greek myth about a young man who saw his own reflection a pool and fell in love with himself. He spent so much time looking at this reflection that he ended up falling in and dying. According to the myth, a flower bloomed where he had fallen in. In modern terms, a person who is described with this term is obsessed with themselves and their own attributes. What is this kind of person called?

4. This is an underground or clandestine market that is usually associated with illegal substances, or noncompliant behavior. This illegal economy can apply to drugs, foreign currency, banned substances, weapons, or in the case of the American prohibition, alcohol. Usually this type of market drives up the value of the item being traded, making illegal traders very wealthy. What is this kind of market called?

5. This Greek island is located in the Cyclades group in the Aegean Sea. It is found between Tinos, Syros, Paros, and Naxos. Its nickname is "the island of the winds," and it is a highly popular tourist destination because of important landmarks and a vibrant nightlife. What is the name of this island?

Answers to Quiz 37

1. Juventus

2. Courteney Cox

3. Narcissist

4. Black market

5. Mykonos

Quiz 38

1. In the USA, The Prohibition Era ran from 1920 to 1933, and was a nationwide ban on alcohol. It was brought into law as an attempt to do away with what were considered morality issues that were being caused by alcohol. The Prohibition gave rise to an illicit trade of alcohol and establishments that sold and served alcohol. They were given their name because people were meant to keep their voices low or not talk about these establishments. What is the name of this kind of establishment?

2. He is an American tennis player who is considered one of the most respected people in the sport. He played professionally from 1988 to 2002, and was known for having a powerful serve so much so that he was nicknamed "Pistol". He has 64 singles titles and held the number 1 position for 286 weeks. He was inducted into the International Tennis Hall of Fame in 2007. What is his name?

3. He is one of the most notorious fictional villains in film and TV, who was most famously portrayed by Anthony Hopkins in The Silence of the Lambs. He was a very intelligent man who was a psychiatrist and a cannibal. He was also portrayed by Mads Mikkelsen and Brian Cox. Most recently, he was the subject of a TV show which also starred Laurence Fishburne. What is this character's name?

4. This is an involuntary contraction (myoclonic jerk) of the diaphragm that may repeat several times per minute. In Latin, it is called singultus for the act of catching one's breath while sobbing. Once triggered, the reflex causes a strong contraction of the diaphragm followed about 0.25 second later by closure of the vocal cords, which results in the sound the contraction is named. Name the contraction.

5. This man was the founder of Playboy magazine, and a former journalist for Esquire. He founded Playboy in 1953, and grew it into the legendary magazine it is today. He was also well-known for living at the Playboy Mansion, and at one point he had three live-in girlfriends who

were the stars of the reality TV series Girls of the Playboy Mansion. He was also famous for donning a robe. What is his name?

Answers to Quiz 38

1. Speakeasy

2. Pete Sampras

3. Hannibal Lecter

4. Hiccup

5. Hugh Hefner

Quiz 39

1. This villain's real name was Tom Marvolo Riddle, and he is often referred to as You-Know-Who", "He-Who-Must-Not-Be-Named", or "the Dark Lord". He is Harry Potter's enemy and the person who is responsible for murdering his parents, James and Lily, who were shielding Harry. Harry is said to have the power to conquer the villain, and the books and movies follow the path to his destruction. What is this character's name?

2. Weather is the state of the atmosphere to the degree that it is hot or cold, wet or dry, calm or stormy, clear or cloudy. Weather refers to day-to-day temperature and precipitation activity in a specific locale. What is the scientific name for the study of the weather?

3. This is an Italian luxury fashion company and trade name founded by a man named Gianni in 1978. The brand produces upmarket Italian-made ready-to-wear and leather accessories. The logo is the head of Medusa, a Greek mythological figure. After Gianni's assassination, the brand was taken over by his sister Donatella, who continued to grow the brand into the giant it is today. One of the most famous dresses designed by this brand is the green plunging neckline dress worn by Jennifer Lopez at the 2000 Grammy Awards. Name this famous fashion house.

4. This is a 1998 American animated film produced by Walt Disney Pictures. The film tells the story of a Chinese warrior's daughter, Fa Mulan, who impersonates a man to take her sick father's place during a war against the Hun dynasty. It is based on a Chinese legend, and the film was considered a departure from Disney's standard princess story and representation. The soundtrack for this film includes Reflection, a song by soon-to-be pop star Christina Aguilera. What was this film's name?

5. Measles is a highly contagious infection that has symptoms like fever, cough, runny nose, small white spots inside the mouth, and red on the face and the body. What is another name for the measles?

Answers to Quiz 39

1. Voldemort

2. Meteorology

3. Versace

4. Mulan

5. Rubella

Quiz 40

1. This fictional villain is the arch nemesis of Batman and an anarchist mastermind who has no empathy and was responsible for bringing chaos to Gotham city. He is identified by wearing clown makeup and sporting a Glasgow smile. He has a dark twisted sense of humor, and is responsible for the murder of Batman's second Robin. He is one of the most famous movie villains of all time, and he generated a lot of fanfare. Heath Ledger's portrayal of this character earned him a posthumous Academy Award, and in Suicide Squad, he was portrayed by Jared Leto. What is the name of this villain?

2. In rock music, where band breakups and disagreements happen so often, it's common for the people who have already found success to team up with musicians from other groups. It's also common for successful solo musicians to come together for one project or to raise money for charity. In most cases this kind of music group happens for a side project. When Guns and Roses and Stone Temple Pilots broke up, Scott Weiland, Slash, and Duff McKagan formed Velvet Revolver. Members of Rage Against the Machine and Soundgarden formed Audioslave. Other examples of this other group are The Dead Weather and Journey. What is this kind of group called?

3. This is an image messaging and multimedia mobile application created by Evan Spiegel, Bobby Murphy, and Reggie Brown, former students at Stanford University. One of the principal concepts of this app is that pictures and messages are only available for a short time. The app is also known for creative filters which include animal faces and other features that can be superimposed over one's face. Name this app.

4. Celebrities are very common victims of this crime, which takes place when a person is so obsessed with someone that they start following them, harassing them, and giving them unwanted attention. The behavior may also escalate to intimidation and even violence, and usually

letters, texts, and phone calls accompany it. In many cases, victims experience this harassment for a very long time until authorities step in. In the late 1980s and 1990s, this behavior began to be classified as a crime. What is the name of this crime?

5. This is a boyband formed in Manchester, England, in the early 90s. The idea of this group was to create a UK version of the wildly successful American group New Kids on the Block. Original members of this group are Gary Barlow, Howard Donald, Mark Owen, Jason Orange, and Robbie Williams. They rose to fame with the single It Only Takes a Minute, and their debut album, Take That and Party. In the mid-90s, they decided to disband, an event which caused distress to so many fans that the government decided to set up a hotline. The band came back as a quartet in 2005, and eventually were rejoined by Robbie Williams. What is the name of this band?

Answers to Quiz 40

1. The Joker

2. Supergroup

3. Snapchat

4. Stalking

5. Take That

Quiz 41

1. This is an instrument used for navigation and direction which originates from China since 206 BC. Originally used in military navigation, it displays markings for angles which correspond to different directions. North corresponds to 0°, east is 90° degrees, south is 180°, and west is 270°. What is the name of this instrument?

2. What is the special name given to the type of coffin Egyptian mummies were put in? The name comes from the Greek words for flesh-eating. They were often made of limestone, and in Ancient Egypt they were elaborate with paintings and decorations, especially the ones that Pharaohs and members of royal families were put in. What is the name of this kind of coffin?

3. She is Colombian actress with nominations for four Golden Globe Awards, four Primetime Emmy Awards, and seven Screen Actors Guild Awards for her portrayal of Gloria Delgado-Pritchett on Modern Family. She started her career co-hosting Spanish television shows, and then she broke into the American market with movies like Chasing Papi and Four Brothers. She is also a successful businesswoman, has been voted one of the most beautiful people alive, and is married to actor Joe Manganiello. Who is this actress?

4. Sheev Palpatine is a fictional character and infamous villain in Star Wars. He is known as the Emperor and the master of Darth Vader, who pulled him over to the dark side. He is responsible for the Clone Wars, almost destroying the Jedi, and creating the Empire. He is killed by Darth Vader, who was trying to save his son, Luke Skywalker. What is Palpatine's other name?

5. During the Paleozoic and Mesozoic eras, the continents of the world were one supercontinent that started to break apart 175 million years ago. Most of the supercontinent was located in the southern hemisphere and was surrounded by a superocean called, Panthalassa. What was the name of this supercontinent?

Answers to Quiz 41

1. Compass

2. Sarcophagus

3. Sophia Vergara

4. Darth Sidious

5. Pangaea or Pangea

Quiz 42

1. On Game of Thrones, this event took place in season 3 on episode 9. It was a massacre that was carried out by Walder Frey but orchestrated by the Lannister family as revenge for Rob Stark breaking up the marriage pact between his house and House Frey. In the attack, King Robb, his pregnant wife, Queen Talisa, his mother, Lady Catelyn, and most of his bannermen and men-at-arms are murdered at a feast. What was the name of this massacre?

2. This is the state of absence of disease activity in patients known to have a chronic illness that cannot be cured. It is commonly used to refer to absence of active cancer or inflammatory bowel disease when these diseases are expected to manifest again in the future. Name this state.

3. In Star Wars, this is a robot character who is featured in the original trilogy, the prequel trilogy, and the sequel trilogy. He is built by Anakin Skywalker and is meant to assist in etiquette and translation. He is a character loved by Star Wars fans because he is funny. He is gold from head to toe. What was this robot's name?

4. Jane Austen's 1813 romance novel, Pride and Prejudice, tells the story of a man with five daughters who cannot inherit any of his property, which means one of them has to marry a wealthy man. When a wealthy man is said to be renting a manor nearby, this causes a stir in the household. When social gatherings occur, they meet the wealthy man's friend Mr. Darcy who is thought to be rude, arrogant, and obnoxious. Eventually the protagonist of the book falls in love with Mr. Darcy. What was the name of this protagonist?

5. Ronald Wilson Reagan was the 40th President of the United States who was in power from 1981 to 1989. He survived an assassination attempt in the 1980s and died in 2004. Before his presidency, he was the 33rd Governor of California from 1967 to 1975. What was his occupation before entering politics?

Answers to Quiz 42

1. The Red Wedding

2. Remission

3. C-3PO

4. Elizabeth Bennett

5. Actor

Quiz 43

1. This is a 2002 romantic comedy starring Jennifer Lopez and Ralph Fiennes. It tells the story of hotel maid who falls in love with a wealthy politician. What is the name of this film?

2. This a Caribbean island country in the Lesser Antilles whose name comes from the Bearded Fig trees that once filled the island. It is situated in the western area of the North Atlantic and is 100 km east of the Windward Islands and the Caribbean Sea. Its capital and largest city is Bridgetown. This is where Rihanna is from. Name this island.

3. Rich Dad, Poor Dad is one of the most popular books about personal finance and wealth building. It shows how to gain financial independence through business ownership, real estate investment, and generally learning to be more responsible with money and making wise decisions when it comes to spending and purchasing. The book's success is also responsible for the development of many workshops that are attended across the world. Who wrote Rich Dad, Poor Dad?

4. This is the secret identity of Don Diego de la Vega, nobleman living in Los Angeles. He wears a black cloak and mask and defends people from villains. He is often portrayed as clever, cunning hero who is always able to outsmart the law and his enemies. He was famously portrayed by Antonio Banderas in a 1998 film and a sequel in 2005. Who is he?

5. This is one of the most watched drama television series in the world. Created by producer Shonda Rhimes, the show is about to enter its 14th season. It follows the story of surgical interns who work at Seattle Grace hospital. The show sees the interns evolve into residents and then attending surgeons who now work at the same hospital, renamed to Grey-Sloan Memorial hospital. Stars of the show include Ellen Pompeo, Patrick Dempsey, Justin Chambers, Jesse Williams, and Debbie Allen. What is the name of this show?

Answers to Quiz 43

1. Maid in Manhattan

2. Barbados

3. Richard Kiyosaki

4. Zorro

5. Grey's Anatomy

Quiz 44

1. This infamous gangster rose to notoriety during the 1930s Prohibition Era as part of what was known as the Chicago Outfit. He was nicknamed Scarface and was born in Brooklyn, New York, to Italian immigrants. He started his criminal career as a bouncer for a gangster who handed the reigns to this guy when he retired. His seven-year reign as crime boss ended when he was 33 years old. He was accused of damaging Chicago's image and was dubbed "Public Enemy No. 1". What was this gangster's name?

2. This is a Netflix show that tells the story of Queen Elizabeth's life, starting with her marriage to Prince Phillip, the death of her father King George VI, and her becoming queen. It also shows the challenges she faced, including her sister, Prince Margaret's controversial relationship with Peter Townsend, unrest in the British colonies, and struggles in her marriage. What is the name of this series?

3. This is a city in the Hejaz region of Saudi Arabia that is also capital of the Makkah Region. The city is located in a narrow valley at a height of 277 m above sea level, and 340 kilometers south of Medina. Its resident population in 2012 was roughly 2 million, although visitors more than triple this number every year during the hajj period held in the twelfth Muslim lunar month of Dhu al-Hijjah. What is this city's name?

4. Chicago is a popular Broadway musical and Oscar-winning film starring Renee Zellweger, Catherine Zeta-Jones, Richard Gere, and Christine Baranski. The story is set in the 1920s jazz era in Chicago, and tells the story of Roxie Hart, an adulteress who shoots her lover. She is imprisoned and hopes to turn her newfound notoriety into fame. In prison, she meets Velma Kelly, a stage performer who murdered her cheating lover and her sister. The two form a rivalry and eventually become stage performers together. One of the main character is the musical is Matron Mama Morton, who is in charge of the prison. Which American rapper and actress played Matron Mama Morton?

5. This is the third album by Canadian singer Alanis Morrissette and the first album released outside Canada. It is a very successful album, and is one of the most important albums of the 20th century. It sold over 33 million units worldwide. You Oughta Know, Hand in my Pocket, You Learn, and Ironic are some of the hits on this album. What is this album called?

Answers to Quiz 44

1. Al Capone

2. The Crown

3. Mecca

4. Queen Latifah

5. Jagged Little Pill

Quiz 45

1. This is one of the three main rock types and is also known as magmatic rock. The other rock types are sedimentary and metamorphic. It is formed through the cooling and solidification of magma or lava. The magma can be derived from partial melts of existing rocks in either a planet's mantle or crust. What is the name of this rock type?

2. The birthstone for January is the garnet, for February it's the amethyst, and for April it's the diamond. May is the emerald, November is the topaz, and December is the ruby. The aquamarine, whose name translates to sea water in Latin, is the birthstone for which month?

3. This online publication and group of news and opinion sites was originally called The Huffington Post, and has since been shortened to HuffPost. It has many divisions, both in the US and across the world. These include politics, business, entertainment, environment, technology, popular media, lifestyle, culture, comedy, healthy living, women's interests, and special subjects like divorce. What is the name of the founder of HuffPost?

4. This is a fairytale about a young, poor boy living with his widowed mother and a dairy cow. When the cow stops giving milk, the boy's mother tells him to take her to the market to be sold. On the way, he meets a man who offers magic beans in exchange for the cow and makes the trade. When his mother discovers what he did, he is punished by going to bed with no supper. She also throws the beans outside the window, and when the boy wakes up the next morning, a giant beanstalk has grown outside of his window. The fairytale features an ogre who says, "fee-fi-fo-fum." What is the name of this fairy tale?

5. Luxury vehicle brand Jaguar was founded as the Swallow Sidecar Company, originally making motorcycle sidecars before developing bodies for passenger cars. The Swallow Sidecar Company was founded by two motorcycle enthusiasts, William Lyons and William Walmsley. In which decade was this car first created?

Answers to Quiz 45

1. Igneous rock

2. March

3. Arianna Huffington

4. Jack and the Beanstalk

5. 1920s (1922)

Quiz 46

1. Quidditch is a sport that is featured in all the Harry Potter books and films. According to Wikipedia, "matches are played between two teams of seven players riding flying broomsticks, using four balls: a Quaffle, two Bludgers, and a Golden Snitch. Six ring-shaped goals are situated atop poles of different heights, three on each side of the pitch." What is the name of the most sought after Quidditch stick?

2. This is a buttery, flaky, French pastry that has a crescent shape. It is made by layering dough with butter and rolling it into the shape. It is a common breakfast food that can also be flavored with chocolate, have sandwich meats put in between or just eaten plain. It a staple of Austrian and French bakeries and pâtisseries. What is the name of this pastry?

3. Saul Hudson is a British-American musician and songwriter. He is a highly talented guitar player who developed a distinct sound when he was the lead guitarist for Guns N Roses. After leaving Guns N Roses, he did his own projects including Snake Pit, and created the group Velvet Revolver. He also wrote a book detailing his rise to fame, his struggle with drug addiction, his marriage, and achieving sobriety. Guns N Roses has since reunited, and he is touring with the group. What is the name of this musician?

4. This is the fifth book of the New Testament which gives a background on the founding of the Christian church after Christ's ascension and the apostles' work spreading the Christian message to the Roman Empire. It also continues the story of Christianity in the 1st century. The book starts with Pentecost and the coming of the Holy Spirit to the Apostles. What is the name of this book?

5. This is a form of alternative medicine developed in Japan. Practitioners use their palms to heal people through universal energy which is transferred from the palms to the person being treated. By harnessing chi, the healing life force, people get better. What is the name of this practice?

Answers to Quiz 46

1. Nimbus 2001

2. Croissant

3. Slash

4. Acts of the Apostles

5. Reiki

Quiz 47

1. What Christian holiday is celebrated on the fiftieth day after Easter? It commemorates the descent of the Holy Spirit upon the Apostles and other followers of Jesus Christ while they were in Jerusalem celebrating the Feast of Weeks. Some Christians believe this event represents the birth of the Church. What is the name of this holiday?

2. This is a state in southeastern United States and a major commercial and cultural center in music and television. The state is the largest east of the Mississippi River, it is home to the city of Atlanta, and famous people like Julia Roberts, Kim Basinger, and CeeLo Green are from this state. It is associated with the peach because of the farming of this fruit. Name this state.

3. This is a fictional household with characters like Gomez and Morticia, Wednesday and Pugsley, close family members Uncle Fester and Grandmama, their butler Lurch, the disembodied hand Thing, and Gomez's Cousin Itt. Based on a comic strip, they can be described as creepy, dark, and obsessed with the macabre. In 1992, the comic strip was adapted into an animated cartoon. What is the name of this clan?

4. This is a British Formula One motor racing team. The team first raced in the 1977 Spanish Grand Prix. They started manufacturing their own cars the following year, and Switzerland's Clay Regazzoni won their first race at the 1979 British Grand Prix. Felipe Massa, Lance Stroll, and Valtteri Bottas are past and present drivers for this team.

5. This is a coastal city in South Africa. It is the second-most populous urban area in South Africa after Johannesburg, and it is also known as the Mother City. It is the seat of the Parliament of South Africa. The city is famous for its well-known landmarks like its harbour, Table Mountain, Signal Hill, and Robben Island. What is the name of this city?

Answers to Quiz 47

1. Pentecost

2. Georgia

3. The Addams Family

4. Williams Martini Racing

5. Cape Town

Quiz 48

1. "Sunrise, Sunset" is a song from which musical? It is performed at a wedding. Two parents sing about how they can't believe their daughter has grown up. Name the musical this song is from.

2. This Vietnamese city used to be known as Saigon. It also used to be called Prey Nokor. It was once part of the French Empire, and then it was annexed by Vietnam in the 17th century. It is the largest city in Vietnam by population. The city's current name is taken from the name of a former Vietnamese leader. What is the name of this city?

3. This was a French painter known as one of the first 19th-century artists to paint modern life in France. He was a pivotal figure in the transition from Realism to Impressionism. His early works, The Luncheon on the Grass, and Olympia, caused great controversy because of their subjects. He is one of the artists who is credited with ushering the transition to modern art and the developments that followed. He died in 1883. What is the name of this painter?

4. This is the 23rd book in the Bible's Old Testament and a book that talks about the church turning its back on God. It also contains prophesies about the birth of Jesus and what his life means for God's people. The book is named after a prophet who was the son of Amoz. He lived in the 8th-century BCE. The book has 66 chapters. Chapter 1–33 promise judgment and restoration for Judah, Jerusalem, and the nations, and chapters 34–66 presume that judgment has been pronounced and restoration follows soon. In Christian circles, it was held in such high regard that is was called "the Fifth Gospel". What is the name of this book?

5. The LBD is an evening or cocktail dress that is considered a wardrobe staple and something that can be worn at different occasions in the day or in the evening. Fashion historians ascribe the origins of this garment to designers like Coco Chanel. It is considered essential to a complete wardrobe, and it is said that every woman should own one. What does LBD stand for?

113

Answers to Quiz 48

1. Fiddler on the Roof

2. Ho Chi Minh City

3. Edouard Manet

4. Isiah

5. Little Black Dress

Quiz 49

1. The "Scramble for Africa" was the event the resulted in the colonization of Africa, and the beginning of New Imperialism. In 1870, only 10 percent of Africa was under European control. By 1914 it had increased to almost 90 percent of the continent. Not all of Africa was colonized. Three modern day countries remained independent. Name one of them.

2. The human skeleton has 206 bones. According to Wikipedia, "it can be divided into the axial skeleton and the appendicular skeleton. The axial skeleton is formed by the vertebral column, the rib cage, the skull, and other associated bones. The appendicular skeleton, which is attached to the axial skeleton, is formed by the shoulder girdle, the pelvic girdle and the bones of the upper and lower limbs." The skeleton can be used to learn a great deal about a human being's life and death, and that is what is studied in forensic anthropology. Name the smallest bone in the body.

3. Monster's Ball is a 2001 American drama film starring Billy Bob Thornton, Heath Ledger, Peter Boyle, Sean Combs, and Mos Def. The film's name is the name given to the last meal of criminals who are on death row and tells the story of three generations of corrections officers. The main character starts a relationship with a woman who turns out to be the widow of a man he executed. Who was the main actress who won an Academy award for this role?

4. This is a style of visual arts, architecture, and design that first appeared in France just before World War I. It influenced the design of buildings, furniture, jewellery, fashion, cars, and movie theatres, and everyday objects such as radios and vacuum cleaners. It combined modernist styles with fine craftsmanship and rich materials. During its heyday, it represented luxury, glamour, exuberance, and faith in social and technological progress.

5. The Italian Grand Prix is one of the longest running events on the Formula One calendar. It and Italian and British Grands Prix are the only Formula One World Championship Grands Prix staged continuously since the championship was introduced in 1950. Where is it held?

Answers to Quiz 49

1. Ethiopia (Abyssinia), the Dervish state (present-day Somalia) and Liberia still being independent.

2. The stapes

3. Halle Berry

4. Art Deco

5. Autodromo Nazionale Monza

Quiz 50

1. This woman was a British stateswoman who was Prime Minister of the United Kingdom from 1979 to 1990 and Leader of the Conservative Party from 1975 to 1990. She was the longest-serving British prime minister of the 20th century and the first woman to have held the office. She was nicknamed The Iron Lady and died on April 8, 2013. What was her name?

2. This is one of the largest hotel brands in the world, founded by a man named Conrad, who was Elizabeth Taylor's first husband. The brand is targeted at both business and leisure travelers with locations in major city centers, near airports, convention centers, and popular vacation destinations around the world. Paris and Nicky are heirs to this brand, what is it called?

3. This is the smallest breed of dog, named after a state in Mexico. They descended from the Techichi, a companion dog favored by the Toltec civilization in Mexico. They are considered feisty, and even though they are the smallest breed of dog, they have the largest-brain body ratio of any breed of dog. The minor league baseball team of El Paso is named after this dog. What is this breed of dog?

4. This author, born on 17 August 1932, is a Nobel Prize-winning British writer who was born in Trinidad. He is known for his comic early novels set in Trinidad and Tobago. He wrote books like A House for Mr. Biswas. What's his name?

5. This is a song written and performed by David Bowie. It is the title track of his third album, which was released in the US in November 1970 and in the UK in April 1971. The persona in the song has an encounter with a doppelgänger. Name this song.

Answers to Quiz 50

1. Margaret Thatcher

2. Hilton

3. Chihuahua

4. V.S Naipaul

5. The Man Who Sold the World

Quiz 51

1. This painter was a founder of French Impressionist painting. According to Wikipedia, he is "the most consistent and prolific practitioner of the movement's philosophy of expressing one's perceptions before nature, especially as applied to landscape painting." The term "Impressionism" is derived from the title of his painting Impression, Sunrise. He also pained Women in the Garden. What was his name?

2. The Jackson 5 is a popular American family music group that was originally known as the Jackson Brothers. Since their start in 1964, they participated in talent shows and performed in clubs, which helped them gain popularity. They entered the professional music scene in 1967, and then signed with Motown in 1969. Michael Jackson got his start in this group and was noticed as a solo talent. Their songs include ABC and Want You Back. Name a member who isn't Michael or Jermaine.

3. Jack Daniel's is probably one of the most famous brands of whiskey in the world which is sold worldwide. It even has new variations including a honey-flavored one. Produced by the Jack Daniel Distillery, the whiskey has come to be associated with one American southern state. What US state is it?

4. This is the capital and most populous city of Mexico, and with a population of over 21 million people, it is the most populous city in the Western Hemisphere and the largest Spanish speaking city in the whole world. Famous people born in this city include Star Wars Rogue One actor Diego Luna and actress Lupita Nyong'o. In 2017, it was hit by a 7.1 magnitude earthquake. What is the name this city?

5. In January 1984, Apple Inc. launched a line of personal computers, the brand's very first mass market computer. Today, this line's products are just known as Mac, and they include the iMac, the Macbook Pro, and the Macbook Air. What was the original name of this computer?

120

Answers to Quiz 51

1. Claude Monet

2. Jackie, Tito, or Marlon

3. Tennessee

4. Mexico City

5. Macintosh

Quiz 52

1. In May 1915, during the First World War, this British warship was sunk by Germany. Making its 202nd crossing from New York to Liverpool, it was torpedoed by a U-boat and was completely underwater in under 20 minutes. 1,198 people died and 761 people survived. The sinking caused great international outcry. What is the name of the ship?

2. This American actor recently turned 54, even though he looks like he's in his 30s! He is best known for his role as Uncle Jesse on the 1990s sitcom Full House, and he also acted in General Hospital as Blackie Parrish. He's had a long-running television career and was once married to model and actress Rebecca Romjin. What is the name of this actor?

3. Romeo and Juliet is a tragedy written by William Shakespeare about two young lovers from feuding families. Set in Verona, Italy, the story follows the meeting of the two young lovers and their ultimate suicides. One of the families was the Montague family, what was the name of their rival family?

4. This is the capital of the Australian state of Queensland. Its metropolitan area has a population of 2.4 million, making it one of the most populous cities in the country. Landmarks in this city include Lone Pine Koala Sanctuary, Queensland Gallery of Modern Art, Sea World Gold Coast, and City Botanic Gardens. Name this city.

5. This small country is located in between Switzerland and Austria. It is a constitutional monarchy ruled by Prince Hans-Adam II. The state is very wealthy, has one of the world's lowest unemployment rates, and gets most of its money from its status as a tax haven. It used to be a part of the Holy Roman Empire and attained its independence in 1719. It was in the German Confederation until 1866. Its capital city is Vaduz, and it became a member of the UN in 1990. What is this country's name?

Answers to Quiz 52

1. Lusitania

2. John Stamos

3. The Capulets

4. Brisbane

5. Liechtenstein

Quiz 53

1. A person from Italy is Italian, a person from London is called a Londoner, a person from California is called a Californian. What word is used for the inhabitants of a place? The name of a people's language is usually the same as this word, for example, the "English" (language or people).

2. Australia is made up on 6 states and 10 territories. It is one of the largest countries in the world in terms of land mass, but most of its relatively small population is located in the coastal areas. The country has over 22 million people, and it is led by Malcolm Turnbull. Three external territories are inhabited; and the others are uninhabited. Every state in Australia is self-governing and also represented in the federal government. Name one of the states in Australia.

3. She is a Colombian singer, songwriter, and dancer best known for songs like Whenever, Wherever, and Hips Don't Lie. She first found success in the Latin music market and then made her successful crossover with her fifth album Laundry Service. She was born in Barranquilla on 2 February 1977. She has two children with football player, Gerard Pique. What is the name of this singer?

4. This is a large-sized breed of dog bred as gun dogs to retrieve shot waterfowl such as ducks and upland game birds during hunting and shooting parties. They have an instinctive love of water, and are easy to train to basic or advanced obedience standards. They are a long-coated breed, with a dense inner coat that provides them with adequate warmth in the outdoors, and an outer coat that lies flat against their bodies and repels water. Name this breed of dog.

5. This is an English-language weekly magazine-format newspaper founded in 1843 by James Wilson. Its offices are located at 25 St. James's Street in Westminster, London. In 2015, its average weekly circulation was over 1.5 million. According to Wikipedia, "the newspaper takes an editorial stance of classical and economic liberalism that supports free trade, globalization, free immigration, and cultural liberalism." What is the name of this magazine?

124

Answers to Quiz 54

1. Demonym

2. Western Australia, Northern Territory, Queensland, Victoria, New South Wales, South Australia, Tasmania

3. Shakira

4. Golden Retriever

5. The Economist

Quiz 55

1. This is an American hip hop group from Staten Island, New York City. The original members of this group are RZA, GZA, Ol' Dirty Bastard, Method Man, Raekwon, Ghostface Killah, Inspectah Deck, U-God, Masta Killa, and Cappadona. Their 1993 debut album is considered to be one of the greatest albums in hip-hop history. What is the name of this group?

2. This is a culinary knife cut in which the food item is cut into long thin strips, similar to matchsticks. Common items are carrots, celery for céléris remoulade, or potatoes for fries. Name this cut.

3. This is a half-size flute and a member of the woodwind family of musical instruments. It has most of the same fingerings as its larger sibling, the standard transverse flute, but the sound it produces is an octave higher than written. Name this instrument.

4. This is the capital of Lebanon and one of the oldest cities in the world, inhabited more than 5,000 years ago. Historically, it was once known as The Paris of the Middle East, and now it is the center of the country's economy and government. Popular places include Mzaar Kfardebian, Sursock museum, and Mohammad Al-Amin Mosque. What is the name of this city?

5. Fireworks are a class of low explosive pyrotechnic devices used for aesthetic and entertainment purposes. They can have effects like noise, light, smoke, and floating materials. Displays are common throughout the world and are the focal point of many cultural and religious celebrations, including New Year's Day, Guy Fawkes, and Diwali. They were invented in the 7th century to scare away evil spirits. In which country were they invented?

Answers to Quiz 55

1. Wu-Tang Clan

2. Julienne

3. Woodwind

4. Beirut

5. China

Quiz 56

1. This is an American rapper, singer, dancer, and record producer who is known as a pioneer in women's hip hop. She is also respected for her highly creative music videos which featured dancing and things like bees. She works a lot with producer Timbaland, and many of her songs feature his distinct sound. She rose to fame in 1997 with the album Supa Dupa Fly, which has singles like *The Rain* and *Sock it to me*. What is the name of this rapper?

2. National French Day is celebrated each year on the 14th of July. The French call it La Fête National. This day celebrates a turning point in the French Revolution and the day the French people were united. People usually celebrate by the Champs Elysees or go for a picnic to drink wine, eat great food, and then watch fireworks displays. What is the name of this event?

3. What is the name of the national anthem of France? It is a song written in 1792 by Claude Joseph Rouget de Lisle in Strasbourg after the declaration of war by France against Austria, and was originally titled "Chant de Guerre Pour l'Armée du Rhin" ("War Song for the Rhine Army"). It was a revolutionary song, an anthem to freedom, a patriotic call to mobilize all the citizens and an exhortation to fight against tyranny and foreign invasion. The French National Convention adopted it as the Republic's anthem in 1795. Name the anthem.

4. This is 1862 French novel written by Victor Hugo. It is also known by many other names including The Wretched Poor. It takes place before and during the French Revolution, telling the story of different people in Paris' poor class. The book was adapted into a musical, and in 2013 a movie starring Hugh Jackman and Anne Hathaway was released. What is the name of this novel and musical?

5. This is a French high fashion luxury goods manufacturer established in 1837. It specializes in leather goods, fragrances, accessories, and fashion. Its logo is of a Duc carriage with horse. It was founded by a

128

man named Thierry, and it was first established as a harness workshop in the Grands Boulevards quarter of Paris, dedicated to serving European noblemen. The brand's current creative director is Nadège Vanhee-Cybulsk, and two of its most sought-after items are the Birkin and Jackie handbags. What is the name of this brand?

Answers to Quiz 56

1. Missy Elliot

2. Bastille Day

3. La Marseillaise

4. Les Misérables

5. Hermes

Quiz 57

1. This is the first single to be released by Lenny Kravitz from an album with the same name. It was released in February 1993. It has the lyrics, "I have come to save the day, and I won't leave until I'm done." Name this song.

2. The US Open is a tournament that takes place towards the end of summer at the Billie Jean King National Tennis Center in Flushing Meadows, New York City. It is the final Grand Slam of each year after the Australian Open, the French Open, and Wimbledon. Who was the 2017 women's champion?

3. This Jewish holiday marks the beginning of the New Year and is the first of the Jewish High Holy Days. Known biblically as Yom Teruah, it usually occurs in the early autumn of the Northern Hemisphere. The holiday is celebrated over two days, starting with the first day of Tishrei, the first month of the Jewish civil year. What is the name of this holiday?

4. In the USA, excellence in writing is awarded with a Pulitzer Prize, excellence in film gets Oscar, a Grammy is for outstanding performance in music, excellence in theatre is awarded with a Tony, and a Golden Globe is won for excellence in film and television. What is the name of the group of awards that celebrate excellence in various parts of television including Daytime, Primetime, and Creative? In 2017, this award show took place on Sunday, September 17. Name this award show.

5. This is a U.S.-based sports channel which screens a wide range of sporting events, including baseball, basketball, ice hockey, and American football. It also screens international sports like football, and features sports commentary and magazine shows. It is one of the most successful sports networks in the world, with shows like Sports Center and Pardon the Interruption. Name this channel.

Answers to Quiz 57

1. Lenny Kravitz

2. Sloane Stephens

3. Rosh Hashanah

4. Emmy Awards

5. ESPN

Quiz 58

1. This is a Cuban-American singer/songwriter who started her career as the lead singer of the Miami Sound Machine. In 1985, she rose to fame and started dominating the charts with the song "Conga". It is her signature song and one of her most successful singles. She also sang the song Reach for the 1996 Olympics, and recently produced a musical based on her life and career called Get on Your Feet. She is married to a man named Emilio, who was a member of her band. What is the name of this singer?

2. This is a type of classical female singing voice which is the highest vocal range of all voice types. In four-part chorale style harmony, this voice takes the highest part, which usually encompasses the melody. Name this singing voice.

3. The Matroska Multimedia Container is an open-source file format that can hold an unlimited number of video, audio, picture, or subtitle tracks in one file. It was created to serve as a universal format for storing multimedia content, like movies or TV shows. What is the file extension for a Matroska file?

4. This is a trilogy of science fiction films by The Wachowski Brothers. It tells the story of a dystopian future in which most human beings live in a simulated reality. Humans being are being controlled by this reality so that their bodies are used as an energy sources by machines. The film's protagonist is a man called Neo, who finds out the truth and becomes part of the group fighting the machines. Stars of the film include, Keanu Reeves, Laurence Fishburne, Carrie-Anne Moss, and Hugo Weaving. What is the name of this film?

5. Mumbai is the capital city of the Indian state of Maharashtra. It is the most populous city in India and one of the most populous cities in the whole world, with an estimated city population of 18.4 million. The name Mumbai is taken from a temple, and it is the entertainment capital of the country because it is where Bollywood is based. It's also

home to the most expensive house in the world and the biggest slum on earth. What was Mumbai's old name?

Answers to Quiz 58

1. Gloria Estefan

2. Soprano

3. MKV

4. The Matrix

5. Bombay

Quiz 59

She was a famous Greek-American soprano who was known all over the world. She was born in New York City and made her debut in Boccaccio. In the 1940s and 1950s, she performed in operas around the world including Italy, Greece, and the US. Before it was shortened, her last name was Kalogeropoulos. She was nicknamed The Tigress because of her diva-like behavior and hot temper. She once stated, "Opera is a battlefield, and it must be accepted." She had an affair with Aristotle Onassis, the man Jackie Kennedy would go on to marry. What was her name?

2. This is the title awarded to a female ballerina who is considered exceptional in talent, and possessing a standard of talent that's higher than her peers. It was given to most notable female ballet dancers, and the term translates to "absolute first ballerina." To be recognized as one is a huge honor, traditionally reserved only for the most exceptional dancers of the generation. What is this title?

3. This is a children's book also known as How Toys Become Real. Written by Margery Williams, it chronicles the story of a stuffed rabbit who wants to come to life through the love of his owner. The book was first published in 1922, and has been republished many times since. Name this book.

4. This is the Hindu festival of lights celebrated every year in autumn in the northern hemisphere and in spring in the southern hemisphere. It is one of the most popular festivals of Hinduism, it spiritually signifies the victory of light over darkness, good over evil, knowledge over ignorance, and hope over despair. Its celebration includes millions of lights shining on housetops, outside doors and windows, and around temples and other buildings in the communities and countries where it is observed. What is the name of this festival?

5. This is a brand of milk chocolate manufactured by Cadbury. Introduced in the United Kingdom in 1905, the range has a number of

products including a Rum and Raisin flavor, a Mint Crisp flavor, and a Wholenut flavor. Sold across the world, all these chocolates are made only with milk chocolate. It is one of the bestselling chocolate bars. What is the name of this chocolate?

Answers to Quiz 59

1. Maria Callas
2. Prima ballerina assoluta
3. The Velveteen Rabbit
4. Diwali or Deepavali
5. Cadbury Dairy Milk

Quiz 60

1. This man was a member of a group of provincial English Catholics who planned the failed Gunpowder Plot of 1605. What was his name?

2. This is an English actor who, in the 1990s, became a poster boy for the romantic comedy genre. He first got international recognition in Four Weddings and a Funeral. He also acted in Mickey Blue Eyes, Notting Hill, and Bridget Jones' Diary. He was also well-known for his relationship with actress Elizabeth Hurley. What is the name of this actor?

3. This is an important Chinese festival celebrated at the turn of the traditional lunisolar Chinese calendar. It is also known as Spring Festival. Celebrations traditionally run from the evening preceding the first day to the Lantern Festival on the 15th day of the first calendar month. The first day of the New Year falls on the new moon between 21 Jan and 20 Feb. What is the name of this holiday?

4. This is an American R&B vocal group from Philadelphia, Pennsylvania, which was discovered by New Edition member Mike Bivins. They are best known for their emotional ballads and *a cappella* harmonies. They were very successful in the 1990s, and nowadays, they perform as a trio composed of baritone Nathan Morris alongside tenors Wanya Morris and Shawn Stockman. Their most successful songs includes "End of the Road", "I'll Make Love to You", and "One Sweet Day". What is the name of this group?

5. This is a song by Michael Jackson and the ninth track on his 1987 album Bad. The song was written and co-produced by Jackson and Quincy Jones. The song has a hard rock sound, and it tells the story of a persistent groupie the singer doesn't like. What is the name of this song?

Answers to Quiz 60

1. Guy Fawkes

2. Hugh Grant

3. Chinese New Year

4. Boyz II Men

5. Dirty Diana

Quiz 61

1. This is a musical charting system that tracks songs that are being purchased and played on radio stations across America and around the world. The chart tabulates songs and albums in various genres including R&B and country, and it also has a general Hot 100 chart that combines singles in all the genres. Albums and songs that break records usually manage to stay on top of the charts for months. What magazine publishes this chart?

2. iTunes is a media player, media library, and online radio broadcaster created by Apple. It can be used on Apple devices and on Windows machines. First released in 2001, the application has now evolved to include a radio service and a charting of popular songs that are being purchased or streamed. In music, what is used to determine the popularity of a song or album on iTunes?

3. This is an American sitcom that aired from 1998-2006. It follows the story of two best friends, one a gay lawyer and the other a straight woman who was an interior designer. Set in New York City, the show also featured their two friends Karen and Jack. The sitcom starred Debra Messing and Will McCormack, and recently it was announced that it will be returning for another season. What was this show's name?

4. This used to describe a word that phonetically imitates, resembles, or suggests the sound that it describes. Common examples include animal noises like oink, roar, or chirp, or sounds like thud, smack, or squelch. What is this called?

5. This American TV series is a popular romantic comedy told in the style of a telenovela. Airing since 2014, it tells the story of religious Latina virgin who gets pregnant after an accidental artificial insemination. The show stars Gina Rodriguez and it won her a Golden Globe in the show's first season. The show features soap opera tropes like evil twins, villains, and complicated love triangles. What is the name of this show?

Answers to Quiz 61

1. Billboard

2. Downloads

3. Will and Grace

4. Onomatopoeia

5. Jane the Virgin

Quiz 62

1. This is an American rock band founded in Little Rock, Arkansas, in 1995 by Amy Lee and Ben Moody. The band first rose to fame with the song Bring Me to Life, which was the official soundtrack for the movie Daredevil. They released their first album, Fallen, in 2003, and it catapulted them into fame. The album won two Grammys and was one of the most successful rock albums of the early 2000s. What is the name of this band?

2. This is a fashion label and lifestyle brand that was launched by musician and mogul Sean Combs, who is more commonly known as Diddy. The company debuted in 1999, and has since run many successful ad campaigns featuring celebrities, won various fashion design awards, and even released a number of fragrances. Its revenue is over $525 million dollars each year. What is this brand's name?

3. This is an English businesswoman, fashion designer, and singer, who rose to fame as Posh Spice. She is married to one of the most famous football players in the world and currently runs a highly successful fashion company. What is this woman's name?

4. This airline is the national carrier for Australia. Founded in 1920, it is one of the oldest airlines in history, which is nicknamed The Flying Kangaroo because of the kangaroo on its logo. The airline is headquartered in Sydney and adopted the name it now uses in 1967. The planes are white and red. It is one of the world's best distance airlines, and subsidiaries include Jetstar Airways and Jetconnect. What is the name of this company?

5. The Hunger Games is a trilogy of novels written by an American novelist. The plot follows two young characters Katniss Everdeen and Peeta Mellark, as they take part in the Hunger Games, a brutal competition that is run by their country's president each year. The novels in the trilogy include Catching Fire and Mockingjay. The novels were adapted into highly successful movies starring actress Jennifer Lawrence, with the film adaptation of Mockingjay split into two parts. Name the author of this trilogy.

Answers to Quiz 62

1. Evanescence

2. Sean Jean

3. Victoria Beckham

4. Shopify

5. Suzanne Collins

Quiz 63

1. This is a martial arts film series directed by Quentin Tarantino. It stars Uma Thurman as a woman out to revenge her attempted murder the deaths of her husband and child. It also stars Lucy Liu, Daryl Hannah, and Keith Carradine. Originally, Tarantino wanted it to be one long film, but it was split into two because it would have been four hours long. What is the name of this film?

2. This is a free and open-source content management system (CMS) based on PHP and MySQL. To function, it has to be installed on a web server, which would either be part of an Internet hosting service or a network host in its own right. It is one of the most common web publishers, and it's also known as WP. What is the name of this CMS?

3. This was a portable music player and media device that was created by Apple. First released in 2001, many versions were released including a Classic which had the distinct wheel that was used to control volume and change songs. There were also smaller versions which were even more portable and a touch version which looked very similar to early models of the iPhone. Since 2017, the Touch is the only one still in production. What is the name of this device?

4. He is a retired German Formula One driver who is best known for driving for Ferrari. He is considered of the best drivers in the history of the sport, having won seven Formula One World Championships. He also holds the records for the most World Championship titles, the most Grand Prix wins, the fastest laps, and the most races won in a single season. What is this man's name?

5. This is a space shuttle disaster that took place on January 28, 1986, in Florida. It took place when a NASA shuttle orbiter mission STS-51-L and the tenth flight of a space shuttle broke apart 73 seconds into its flight, killing all seven crew members. The spacecraft disintegrated over the Atlantic Ocean, and remains one of the worst accidents to happen in the US. What was the name of the shuttle that crashed?

Answers to Quiz 63

1. Uma Thurman

2. Wordpress

3. iPod

4. Michael Schumacher

5. Challenger

Quiz 64

1. He was one of the richest men in the world with a shipping company and the world's largest privately-owned shipping fleet. He was Greek and Argentine, and was known for his wealth and personal life, which included marrying Jackie Kennedy after the death of JFK. What was this man's name?

2. This is a lightly scented cologne used as a skin freshener, which is also called aromatic waters or flower water. It is used to refer to how strong a fragrance is, and it is usually applied directly to the skin after bathing or shaving. It is weaker than Eau de Parfum and stronger than Eau de Cologne. What is this called?

3. This is a cat that appears in Lewis Carroll's story Alice in Wonderland. It is known for its distinctive mischievous grin. One of its distinguishing features is that from time to time its body disappears, the last thing visible being its iconic grin. Name this cat.

4. This historic event which took place in 1929 was also known as Black Tuesday. It was the most devastating stock market crash in the history of the United States. It was the beginning of the 12-year Great Depression that affected all Western industrialized countries. Name this event.

5. This politician was the president of Venezuela from 1999 to 2013, when he died of cancer. He was also a revolutionary who led the Fifth Republic Movement political party from 1997 until 2007. When he was younger, he wanted to be a baseball player, but he became a soldier instead. In 2002, he temporarily lost his seat as President after a coup. He even used to host his own television show. What was this man's name?

Answers to Quiz 64

1. Aristotle Onassis

2. Eau De Toilette

3. The Cheshire Cat

4. Wall Street Crash

5. Hugo Chavez

Quiz 65

1. This a large bag with parallel handles that emerge from its sides. Common fabrics include heavy canvas, possibly dyed, or treated to resist moisture and mold. Name this kind of bag.

2. This is a fashion house and luxury retail company founded in 1854. The label's LV monogram appears on most of its products, which are mainly luxury trunks and other pieces of luggage. The brand also evolved into creating ready-to-wear fashion looks, couture looks, as well as shoes and other accessories. Actress Michelle Williams and tennis legends Steffi Graf and Andre Agassi are just a few names who have appeared in campaigns for this company. What is its name?

3. This is a 2015 action film co-written, co-produced, and directed by George Miller. It is the fourth installment and a reboot of the Mad Max franchise. The film is set in a future desert wasteland where gasoline and water are scarce commodities. It follows Max Rockatansky, who joins forces with Imperator Furiosa to flee from cult leader Immortan Joe and his army in an armored tanker truck. The film starred Tom Hardy and Charlize Theron, and it won many awards for costume design. What is the name of this film?

4. This is a country in the Horn of Africa, which won its independence from Ethiopia in 1993. Major languages in this country include Tigrinya, Tigre, Arabic, and English. Its capital city is Asmara, and it is bordered by Sudan, Ethiopia, and Djibouti. The northeastern and eastern parts of the country have an extensive coastline along the Red Sea. What is the name of this country?

5. This is a type of bacon sandwich made up of bacon, lettuce, tomato, and bread. It evolved from the tea sandwiches served at a similar time to the club sandwich. What is the abbreviated name of this type of sandwich?

Answers to Quiz 65

1. Tote bag

2. Louis Vuitton

3. Mad Max: Fury Road

4. Eritrea

5. BLT

Quiz 66

1. This is an American novelist, currently the bestselling author alive and the fourth bestselling fiction author of all time. She was born in New York City in 1947. She is the fourth-bestselling fiction author of all time. Her novels all revolve around wealthy families going through a difficult time. Name this author.

2. This was a Southern African state that existed from 1965 to 1979. Founded by Cecil John Rhodes' British South Africa Company, the former British territory had its capital at Salisbury. In 1980 the country attained its independence and became Zimbabwe. What was the colonial name of this country?

3. The Allegory of the Cave was presented to compare "the effect of education and the lack of it on our nature". It is written as a dialogue between the author's brother and his mentor. The allegory is presented after the analogy of the sun and the analogy of the divided line. Who wrote this allegory?

4. What is the deliberate killing of a person of royalty called? According to Wikipedia, "In the British tradition, it refers to the judicial execution of a king after a trial. More broadly, it can also refer to the killing of an emperor or any other reigning sovereign." What is it called?

5. A papal conclave is used to elect a new Pope or Bishop of Rome. It is held at the Sistine Chapel, and ballots are cast to determine who will get the role. Recently, we saw this event happen when Pope Benedict XVI resigned and Pope Francis was voted in as pope. The process of the conclave is that ballots are cast, and when the vote fails to come up with a pope, ballots are burnt, and black smoke can be seen from a chimney outside. When they finally have a pope, the chimney emits white smoke. What is the name of the group that officially elects the pope?

Answers to Quiz 66

1. Danielle Steele

2. Rhodesia

3. Plato

4. Regicide

5. College of Cardinals

Quiz 67

1. This is an American novelist, short story writer, poet, and activist. She wrote the critically acclaimed novel The Color Purple for which she won the National Book Award and the Pulitzer Prize for Fiction. She also wrote the novels Meridian and The Third Life of Grange Copeland. Name this novelist.

2. This is a dessert made of layers of filo pastry which is sweetened and filled with chopped nuts and further sweetened with syrup or honey. It originated from parts of Europe, as well as Central and West Asia. What is the name of this pastry?

3. She is a model from the 1960s Mod era who gained her nickname for her stick thin build. Born Lesley Hornby in 1949, she became a cultural icon in England and became the face of an important fashion and cultural movement. She was known for a very trendy cropped blonde haircut, and ended up becoming an actress in films like The Boy Friend, The Blues Brothers, and Madame Sousatzka. What was this model's nickname?

4. This is a cosmetic commonly used to enhance the eyelashes. It may darken, thicken, lengthen, and/or define the eyelashes. Normally in one of three forms—liquid, cake, or cream—the modern mascara product has various formulas; however, most contain the same basic components of pigments, oils, waxes, and preservatives. Name this product.

5. This is a 1992 American animated musical fantasy film produced by Walt Disney Feature Animation for Walt Disney Pictures. The film follows a street urchin who finds a magic lamp containing a genie. He gets a flying carpet and ends up falling in love with Jasmine, a sultan's daughter. A Whole New World, is one of the songs from this film. What is the name of this film?

Answers to Quiz 67

1. Alice Walker

2. Baklava

3. Twiggy

4. Mascara

5. Aladdin

Quiz 68

1. He is an American author who is one of the most successful novelists of all time. He is best known for his crime novels, with works like Alex Cross, Michael Bennett, Women's Murder Club, Maximum Ride, Daniel X, NYPD Red, Witch and Wizard, and the Private series. What is his name?

2. This is the highest mountain in Africa and a dormant volcano. It has three volcanic cones, Kibo, Mawenzi, and Shira, and it rises approximately 4,900 meters from its base to 5,895 meters above sea level. According to reports, about 35,000 people attempt to climb its peaks each year, but only 2/3 are able to do it, with the rest turning back. Name this mountain.

3. This is both a carnivorous and an herbivorous feeding behavior in which an animal feeds on the remains of dead animals that have already been eaten and left by predators. Common animals that have this behavior are vultures, hyenas, and raccoons. What is it called?

4. This is a major international sporting event held once every four years for ice sports. Starting in 1924, the very first event of this kind took place in Chamonix, France. The original five sports were bobsleigh, curling, ice hockey, Nordic skiing, and skating. The most recent games were held in Sochi, Russia, in 2014. Name these games.

5. This is an online news and social networking service where users post and interact with messages restricted to 140 characters. It is considered one of the most important apps of the Web 2.0 age, and it also changed the culture of storytelling and news. This app also made the use of hashtags more popular in social media and spun other apps like Vine and Periscope. Founded by Jack Dorsey, Noah Glass, Evan Williams, and Biz Stone, the company is based in San Francisco, California. Name this social network.

Answers to Quiz 68

1. James Patterson

2. Mount Kilimanjaro

3. Scavenging

4. Winter Olympics

5. Twitter

Quiz 69

1. This is the largest city in the United Arab Emirates (UAE). It is on the southeast coast of the Persian Gulf and is the capital of one of the seven emirates. It's most popular landmarks are the Burj Al Arab and the Burj Khalifa, a 160-story skyscraper. What is the name of this city?

2. This is an alcoholic beverage produced from grapes grown in the Champagne region of France. The term is mainly used to describe the wine only when it's produced in that particular region, but some people apply the term to all wines that have particular characteristics. What is the name given to this drink when it isn't produced in the Champagne region?

3. He is a Canadian singer and songwriter and one of the most famous young pop stars of our age. After he was discovered through his YouTube videos covering songs, he released his first studio album, My World 2.0, in 2010, which had the hit single "Baby". He has since performed songs such as What Do You Mean, Love Yourself, and Somebody to Love. What is this singer's name?

4. This is a line of wearable technology products that tracks heart rate, quality of sleep, and steps climbed. These activity trackers are wireless-enabled and use Bluetooth to connect to mobile devices. The product range includes the Blaze, Charge, Surge, and Alta. What is this brand's name?

5. This is considered to be one of the oldest types of pasta. It is flat shaped, and the dish it makes is made with several layers of sheets alternated with sauces and other ingredients, such as minced beef. What is this pasta called?

Answers to Quiz 69

1. Dubai

2. Sparkling Wine

3. Justin Bieber

4. Fitbit

5. Lasagne

Quiz 70

1. This alcoholic beverage traces its history and creation to Eastern Europe in the 9th century. It is a mixture of water and ethanol, and it can also have traces of impurities and flavorings added to it. Its name is taken from the Russian word for water. Traditionally, it is made by the distillation of cereal grains or potatoes that have been fermented. What is the name of this beverage?

2. This is the capital and largest city of Ireland which was originally founded as a Viking settlement. Its name comes from the Gaelic word meaning "black pool," and it was at one point the second largest city in the British Empire. In this city, you can find the Guinness storehouse, Phoenix Park, and St Stephens Green. The band U2 is from this city, and actor Colin Farrell, Oscar Wilde, and Conor McGregor all come from this city. What is the name of this city?

3. In politics and governance, this is a direct vote in which an entire electorate has to vote on a particular issue or proposal. This may result in the adoption of a new law. It was carried out in the UK to determine whether to stay in the EU or leave. What is this process called?

4. This is the tenth astrological sign in the zodiac. Represented by the goat, the star sign runs from 21 December to 19 January. It belongs to the earth element, and people under this sign are known to be achievers, struggling to reach concrete results. What is this sign?

5. This Eurasian nation used to be center of the very powerful Ottoman Empire. It being between Europe and Asia makes it hold a major strategic and cultural role. It has 13 UNESCO World Heritage sites, which is one of many reasons it's one of the most visited cities in the world by tourists. It is bordered by Greece, Bulgaria, Georgia, Armenia, Nakhchivan, Iran, Iraq, and Syria. The country is surrounded by the Aegean Sea, the Black Sea, and the Mediterranean Sea. Ankara is the capital, and Istanbul is the country's largest city and main cultural and commercial centre. Its current leader is Recep Tayyip Erdoğan, and

points of interest include, Hagia Sophia, Pamukkale, and Sultan Ahmed Mosque. What is this country called?

Answers to Quiz 70

1. Vodka

2. Dublin

3. Referendum

4. Capricorn

5. Turkey

Quiz 71

1. This is an American RnB/hip hop female group from Atlanta Georgia. They rose to fame in the 1990s with their album Crazy, Sexy, Cool. The group was originally made up of Tionne "T-Boz" Watkins, the late Lisa "Left Eye" Lopes, and Rozonda "Chilli" Thomas. The group now performs as a duo and released a single called Way Back in 2017. What is this group's name?

2. This so-called haunted area is located in the western part of the Northern Atlantic Ocean between Florida and Puerto Rico. It is called the Devil's Triangle because it has been the site of the disappearance of ships and planes. It has become quite a mysterious area and has led to many legends and myths being formed around it. What is the more common name of this area?

3. Prince Phillip, or the Duke of Edinburgh, is the husband of Queen Elizabeth II and the father of Prince Charles. He comes from a line of Danish, Greek, and Norwegian royals, but he became a naturalized British citizen when he got married to the then Princess Elizabeth. What is the last name he took up when he became British?

4. This popular game requires players to match descending tiles into a puzzle like structure. Designed by Russian game designer Alexey Pajitnov, the name of the game comes from the Greek word for the pieces. The game is very popular on mobile devices. What is the name of this game?

5. This federation was formed after World War II and was made up of what is now Croatia, Slovenia, Serbia, Bosnia, Hercegovina, Montenegro, Macedonia, and Kosovo. The federation existed until 1992. What was the name of this federation?

Answers to Quiz 71

1. TLC

2. Bermuda Triangle

3. Mountbatten

4. Tetris

5. Yugoslavia

Bonus Questions 1:
World Leaders

1. The Democratic Republic of Congo is a Central African state that is bordered by Central African Republic, South Sudan, Uganda, Rwanda, Burundi, Tanzania, Zambia, Angola, and the Republic of the Congo. It is a former colony of Belgium and was officially renamed to the Democratic Republic of Congo in 1964. In 1997, the country's third president overthrew the former leader whose leadership was associated with corruption. On January 16, 2001 he was assassinated by one of his bodyguards, and his son Joseph took over from him. This man was born in Belgian Congo in 1939 and attained his university education in France. Upon his return to Congo, he entered politics and formed the People's Revolutionary Party. What was this man's name?

2. This politician is the 23rd and current Prime Minister of Canada. He is also the leader of the Liberal Party and the second child in Canadian history who was born to a sitting Prime Minister. When he delivered the eulogy for his father, he rose to fame and prominence. He assumed office as Prime Minister in 2015, after the end of Stephen Harper's time as Prime Minister. He has gained worldwide respect and admiration for upholding human rights and being outspoken against injustice. What is his name?

3. This former US president was born William Jefferson Blythe III on the 19 of August 1946. When he was young, he met John F. Kennedy at the White House, and that was an event that inspired him to want to work in public affairs. He later attended Yale Law School where he met his wife who also became a prominent politician. He became the 40th Governor of Arkansas, and then he became the 42nd president of the United States in 1992. At the time of his election, he was the 3rd youngest president in US history. His presidency was mired in scandal when he was accused of having an affair with a White House intern, Monica Lewinsky. The scandal eventually died down, and the man

enjoys a great legacy and a lucrative public speaking career. What is this man's name?

4. This Palestinian politician was born Abdel-Rahman Abdel-Raouf Arafat al-Qudwa al-Husseini on October 24, 1929, in Cairo. He was the Executive Chairman of the Palestine Liberation Organization (PLO) from 1969 to 2004 and President of the Palestinian National Authority (PNA) from 1994 to 2004. From his youth, he was an active supporter of the Palestinian cause. He studied engineering in Egypt, created a student union, and became a founding member and long serving leader of Fateh. He became a prominent face in the ongoing relations between Israel and Palestine, and once stated, "I come bearing an olive branch in one hand and the freedom fighter's gun in the other. Do not let the olive branch fall from my hand." He always wore a Keffiyeh, a headscarf typically worn by Arab people. He died in 2004. What was this man's name?

5. This English politician and statesman was the leader of the Labour Party from 1940 to 1955. He was Prime Minister of Great Britain, in office between 1951 and 1955, and served two monarchs, Queen Elizabeth II and her father George VI. He was preceded by Neville Chamberlain and succeeded by Anthony Eden. He was a very influential man who led Britain through the difficulties of the Second World War and through the colonial uprisings in different parts of the British Empire. In 1953, he won the Nobel Prize in Literature. He died at age 90 in 1965. He once said, "We make a living by what we get, but we make a life by what we give." What was this man's name?

6. This is a French politician was born on January 28, 1955. Born in Paris, he served as the President of France and ex officio Co-Prince of Andorra from 16 May 2007 until 15 May 2012. Before his presidency, he was the leader of the Union for a Popular Movement (UMP) party. During Jacques Chirac's second presidential term he served as Minister of the Interior. He was also mayor of Neuilly-sur-Seine, one of the wealthiest areas in France. He is married to actress and model Carla Bruni. What is his name?

7. This was a Soviet revolutionary and political leader who ruled the Soviet Union from the mid-1920s until 1953. Under his leadership, the union became a dominant global power, and he even had a city named after him. He was actually from Georgia, and his Marxist views helped

him rise up the ranks in the Soviet government after he was expelled from his native country. He once said, "a single death is a tragedy; a million deaths is a statistic." He rose up the ranks of the Communist Party, becoming General Secretary of the Central Committee of the Communist Party of the Soviet Union from 1922 to 1952, eventually taking control of the whole party. He died in 1953. What was his name?

8. He was the President of Uganda from 1971 to 1979, and was known to be a ruthless leader. He rose up in the Ugandan military after the nation gained its independence from Britain. In 1965, he was made commander of the army, and in the early 1970s, he orchestrated a military coup which allowed him to become president. He died in August 2003 in Saudi Arabia. He was portrayed by Forrest Whittaker in the 2006 historical film, The Last King of Scotland. What was his name?

9. He was a Filipino politician born in 1917. He ruled the Philippines from 1965 to 1986. His regime was associated with a high amount of corruption, and he was known as a kleptocrat who amassed a great deal of wealth and lived a very extravagant life during which he brutalized his people. He died on the 28 September 1989, in Honolulu, Hawaii. What was his name?

10. He was an Italian politician and the leader of the National Fascist Party. Born in Predappio, Italy, in 1883, he was once a member of the Socialist Party but abandoned this ideal when he was expelled from the party during the First World War. After forming the Fascist movement, he eventually became the Italian Prime Minister from 1922 to 1925. He then set up a dictatorship and became known as Il Duce. He once said, "Democracy is beautiful in theory; in practice, it is a fallacy." What was this man's name?

11. He was the supreme leader of the Democratic People's Republic of Korea from 1994 to 2011, and the predecessor to the current leader, his son. He also succeeded his own father. He was born Yuri Irsenovich Kim in 1941 in the Soviet Union. By the early 1980s, he had become the heir apparent for the leadership of the DPRK, and when his father died in 1994, he was named supreme leader. He oversaw one of the biggest armies in the world, and he studied politics and economics. In 2011, he died in Pyongyang. What was his name?

12. He was an Israeli general and statesman who served as the 11th Prime Minister of Israel from March 2001 until April 2006. His nickname was Arik, and he was very active in the Israeli War of Independence in 1948. He was incapacitated by a stroke in January 2006 and died in 2014. What was this leader's name?

13. This is a Ghanaian diplomat who was born in Kumasi, and served as the seventh Secretary-General of the United Nations from January 1997 to December 2006. In 2001, he was awarded the Nobel Peace Prize for the work he did with the UN. Currently, he is the Chairman of The Elders, an international organization founded by Nelson Mandela. What is his name?

14. He was President of the Democratic Republic of the Congo from 1965 to 1997. He was born in the DRC in 1930, and rose through the ranks of the military, becoming Patrice Lumumba's secretary. He became chief of staff of the army and eventually rose to power. As President, he amassed a lot of money and became known for a very lavish lifestyle, which included a large and ornate palace. He is said to have embezzled up to US$14 billion dollars during his time as leader, and he also became known for his authoritarian rule. He died in 1997 in Morocco. What was his name?

15. He was the fifth President of Iraq and a prominent member of the Arab Socialist Ba'ath Party. Born in 1937, he ruled the Muslim nation from 16 July 1979 until 9 April 2003. During his leadership, he built a strong military that he had a lot of influence over, and he was accused of running a ruthless dictatorship. His presidency came to an end during the US invasion of Iraq. After going into hiding, he was found, captured, and eventually executed. What was his name?

16. He was a Panamanian politician and CIA informant who ruled Panama from 1983 to 1989. Born in 1934, he rose through the ranks of the Panamanian army, and when he eventually consolidated power and became the leader of the nation, he was said to have run a dictatorship. He also worked closely with the CIA providing high level intelligence. Eventually, he was removed from power by the United States. He died in May 2017, following complications from a brain surgery.

17. He was a Yugoslav and Serbian politician and the President of Serbia from 1989 to 1997 and President of Yugoslavia from 1997 to 2000.

Born in 1941, in Nazi-occupied Serbia, he became a leader of the Socialist Party in that country. After rising to power, his presidency was subject to criticism because it seemed that he was aiming to strengthen the position of Serbs at the expense of Kosovo Albanians. This led to great unrest in Yugoslavia. Towards the end of his presidency, he was charged with war crimes including genocide and crimes against humanity. He died in 2006 in The Hague. What was his name?

18. He was the leader of Malawi from 1961 to 1994. Born in 1898, in what was then the British Central Africa Protectorate, he received most of his education in the United States, returning to the country to push for liberation from British Imperialism. In 1963, he was formally appointed prime minister of Nyasaland, and under his leadership, the country saw a great deal of development and even the advancement of women's rights. In 1964, Malawi became independent, and eventually he declared himself President for Life. His regime was accused of brutality and violence against political opponents. He died in 1997 in South Africa. What was his name?

19. He was a Libyan politician and political theorist who was born between 1940 and 1943, in what was then Italian Libya. He governed Libya as Revolutionary Chairman of the Libyan Arab Republic from 1969 to 1977, then as the "Brotherly Leader" of the Great Socialist People's Libyan Arab Jamahiriya from 1977 to 2011. He enrolled in the military as a youth and became an Arab nationalist. In 1969, he took power in a coup and nationalized various parts of the country's economy. The country became a Jamahiriya, a type of socialist state. The country became isolated from the rest of the world and was one of the countries affected by the Arab Spring Uprisings. During this revolution, he was captured and executed. What was this man' name?

20. She is the 66th United States Secretary of State, the first African-American woman to hold the post, as well as the second woman and second African-American. Born in 1954, she served under President George W. Bush and earlier in her career worked as a European Affairs advisor during the dissolution of the Soviet Union and the reunification of Germany. From 1993 to 1999, she was provost of Stanford University. What is her name?

21. She is the queen consort of Jordan and a philanthropist. Born in 1970 in Kuwait to a Palestinian family, she met Prince Abdullah after

she moved to Jordan to work. She has a degree in Business Administration from the American University in Cairo and worked at Citibank. She became queen in 1999, and since becoming Princess, she put a lot of work into advancing areas like education, health, and community empowerment across the globe.

22. This is a British politician who served as Prime Minister of the United Kingdom from 1997 to 2007 and Leader of the Labour Party from 1994 to 2007. Born in 1953, he became a Labour Party member soon after graduating from university, and eventually became the Member of Parliament (MP) for Sedgefield. When John Smith, the leader of the Labour Party, died, he came party leader. He once said, "Power without principle is barren, but principle without power is futile." What is his name?

Answers to Bonus Questions 1: World Leaders

1. Laurent Kabila

2. Justin Trudeau

3. Bill Clinton

4. Yasser Arafat

5. Winston Churchill

6. Nicolas Sarkozy

7. Joseph Stalin

8. Idi Amin

9. Ferdinand Marcos

10. Benito Mussolini

11. Kim Jong-il

12. Ariel Sharon

13. Kofi Annan

14. Mobutu Sese Seko

15. Saddam Hussein

16. Manuel Noriega

17. Slobodan Milošević

18. Hastings Kamuzu Banda

19. Muammar Gaddafi

20. Condoleezza Rice

21. Queen Rania

22. Tony Blair

Bonus Questions 2:
Notable People in History

1. She was a world-famous aviator who was the first woman to fly across the Atlantic Ocean solo. She has set many other world records and was a pioneer in aviation for women. She disappeared in 1937, during an attempt to fly across the globe, and was never found again. What was her name?

2. He was the king of England from 11 December 1936 to 6 February 1952, and the father of the current Queen, Elizabeth II. He became king after the abdication of his older brother, Edward VIII who decided not to become king when he wasn't allowed to marry a divorcee. His real name was Albert, but that wasn't the name he chose to use when he became king. He died in 1952 after a battle with lung disease, and his eldest daughter took over at age 25. What was his name as King?

3. He was the last king of France before the French Revolution and the changes to the French rulership and democracy. He was born Louis-Auguste and held the throne until the monarchy was removed in 1792. The revolution was caused by massive discontent among the country's lower and middle classes and what was seen as abuse of power and resources. The king and his wife, Marie Antoinette, were seen as the face of the French monarchy, and that led to their beheadings. What was this king's name?

4. He was a military leader who rose to political power in the French Revolution, eventually becoming Emperor of France from 1804-1815. Even though he had no formal military training, he is considered a military genius whose military tactics are still discussed today. He led a great many military battles for France, gaining a lot of respect from other parts of the world. A common rumor about him that he was really short actually isn't grounded in any fact and was the result of propaganda. His army was responsible for the discovery of the Rosetta Stone, and ultimate-

ly, he was exiled to St. Helena. What was this man's name?

5. He was the last Emperor of Russia, ruling from the age of 26 after his grandfather was assassinated and his father died after ascending to the throne. He ruled from 1894 to 1917, when he had to abdicate the throne during the 1917 revolution. He was nominated for a Nobel Peace Prize in 1901, but during his reign, the Russian Empire collapsed. What was this king's name?

6. She was an Egyptian queen and the wife of Akhenaten. Her name means "the beautiful one has come," and her bust is probably one of the most common things we associate with Ancient Egypt. She is considered one of the most powerful women of ancient Egypt who, along with her husband, ruled Egypt during a time of great wealth and prosperity. She and Akhenaten were also central to the cult of Aten. What was her name?

7. This biblical character is mentioned in the Book of Genesis in the story of Joseph, who went from favorite son to slave and then eventually to a close counsel of the king. During Joseph's days as a slave, he was employed by a man who was thought to be the captain of the palace guard. After being made the head of this man's household, his wife made advances at Joseph, and when he turned her down she accused him of rape, and he was subsequently imprisoned. What was the name of the man that employed Joseph?

8. She is one of the most iconic rulers of the British Empire, who ruled for more than 60 years. When she was born, she was fifth in line for the throne, but at 18, she surprisingly became queen after her uncle died with no direct heirs to take the throne. Her mother was the Duchess of Kent, and her rule started the royal line of Saxe-Coburg and Gotha. She is also known as the Grandmother of Europe because her children all married into royal families across the continent. What was this Queen's name?

9. He was a British mining magnate and a British imperialist who founded Rhodesia, a British colony that is now present-day Zambia and Zimbabwe. He was also Prime Minister of the Cape Colony, and to this day the South African city Cape Town holds many references to him including statues, memorials, and a great deal of land. Another South African university, in Grahamstown is named after him. He was

the owner of the British South Africa Company, and he had the dream of constructing a railway that went from Cape to Cairo. When he died, he was buried in Rhodesia. What was this man's name?

10. King Henry VIII had six wives, and this woman is probably one of the most famous ones. When she became his second wife, the king rejected Catholicism and founded the Anglican Church because he wouldn't have been able to divorce his first wife. Even though the king had had an affair with her sister, he ended up marrying her, and she gave birth to the woman who would eventually become Queen Elizabeth I. When she couldn't give him a son, Henry VIII began an affair with Jane Seymour. She was eventually imprisoned and executed for adultery, which was considered an act of treason. What was her name?

11. This man was the founder of the Mongol Empire, who only got his name in 1206 after becoming a prominent leader. He endured a difficult childhood and youth and then came to power by uniting many of the nomadic tribes of Northeast Asia. He conquered a huge part of what is now Eurasia. By the end of his life, the Mongol Empire occupied a substantial portion of Central Asia and China. What was this man's name?

12. He was one of the most influential monarchs of the Zulu Kingdom and Southern Africa. He was a great military leader who was known for his tough, strict rules including restricting his soldiers from getting married. When his mother died, he declared a year-long mourning period. He was born near present-day Melmoth, KwaZulu-Natal Province in South Africa. What was his name?

13. He was a child protege and composer who was so brilliant he was playing music as young as age five and performing at royal courts not long after. He was very influential, and he composed more than 600 works in his lifetime. Born in Salzburg Austria, he composed his first symphony at the age of eight, and later on when he had a position playing at the royal court, he decided to pursue an independent career. Pope Clement XIV awarded him the Order of the Golden Spur. He died in 1971, from a mysterious illness which some believe was the result of a poisoning by a rival. What was his name?

14. This was a German composer and pianist, and a very important composer in the transition between Classical and Romantic music. He

remains one of the most famous and influential of all composers whose symphonies have become standards in Classical music training. His best-known compositions include 9 symphonies, 5 piano concertos, 1 violin concerto, 32 piano sonatas, 16 string quartets, and one opera, Fidelio. Many of his works were composed when he was deaf. What was his name?

15. This man was a French fashion designer who is considered a great pioneer in women's fashion. He and Coco Chanel are considered as two of the most important designers in the twentieth century. He brought a new energy and great ideas to women's fashion, caring about both comfort and elegance. He is known for also introducing the tuxedo suit for women and was known for his use of non-European cultural references. He died in 2008, but left behind a great legacy and a powerful fashion house that is still loved today. What was his name?

16. This legendary American soul singer and performer was nicknamed the Godfather of Soul for his contribution to the development of the genre. He is also a pioneer of funk music whose songs have been sampled in many hip hop songs. Born in South Carolina in 1933, he rose to fame starting with singing gospel and then building a career that lasted six decades. He performed at the Rumble in the Jungle, the historic boxing match between George Foreman and Muhammad Ali. His greatest hits include, "Papa's Got a Brand New Bag", "I Got You (I Feel Good)" and "It's a Man's Man's Man's World". What was this musician's name?

17. He was an American inventor and businessman who has been described as America's greatest inventor. He developed many devices that greatly influenced life around the world, including the phonograph, the motion picture camera, and the long-lasting, practical electric light bulb. He was one of the first inventors to apply the principles of mass production and large-scale teamwork to the process of invention, and because of that, he is often credited with the creation of the first industrial research laboratory. What was this man's name?

18. This legendary children's novelist and short story writer was born in 1916 in Cardiff, United Kingdom. His stories became well known in the 1914, writing works like James and the Giant Peach, Charlie and the Chocolate Factory, Matilda, The Witches, Fantastic Mr. Fox, and The BFG. He is considered one of the greatest children's storytellers of the

20th century and he came to be known for dark comedy and macabre style in his writing. He died in 1990, and left a great legacy and stories that have even been adapted into movies and cartoons. His granddaughter, Sophie, is a well-known British model and author. What was his name?

19. She was a children's storyteller and novelist born in London in 1897. She was one of the bestselling writers of the 20th century with more than 600 million copies sold. She wrote on a wide range of topics including education, natural history, fantasy, mystery, and biblical narratives. Her work includes the Noddy, Famous Five, Secret Seven, Adventure, and Malory Towers series. What was her name?

20. He was born Reginald Kenneth Dwight, and he is a legendary English singer, pianist, and composer who has been active for decades. He is also iconic because of his costumes and funky wardrobe choices for the stage. He has more than fifty Top 40 hits, and is the eighth-highest-certified music artist in the US. He originally wrote the song Candle in the Wind for Marilyn Monroe, but when Princess Diana died in 1997, he reworked it. His other songs include Rocket Man, Tiny Dancer, and Don't Go Breaking My Heart. He is also a gay rights activist who has raised money for HIV/AIDS initiatives and was knighted in 1998. What is his name?

21. This man was an English Anglican cleric and theologian who is the founder of the United Methodist Church, which he built with his brother Charles and fellow cleric George Whitefield. He was a highly educated man who wrote a bestselling medical text and coined the term "agree to disagree". He left the Church of England after the American Revolution. What was his name?

22. This holy man was born Karol Józef Wojtyła and was the pope and bishop of Rome from 1978 to 2005. He was elected in 1978, after his predecessor, who had been elected to succeed Pope Paul VI, died after thirty-three days as pope. Cardinal Wojtyła was elected on the third day of the conclave and adopted his predecessor's name in tribute to him. He has a great legacy which includes helping end Communism in Poland, improving Catholic relations with Judaism, Islam, the Eastern Orthodox Church, and the Anglican Communion. He was beatified on 1 May 2011, after many people came forward about the miracles he performed. He also survived as assassination attempt in 1981. What was this man's name?

23. She was an American actress who won four Academy Awards for films including Guess Who's Coming to Dinner, The Lion in Winter, and On Golden Pond. She was very independent, outspoken, and considered ahead of her time in terms of her views on women's rights. She even started wearing pantsuits before it was widely accepted for women to. She had a long career, working in Hollywood for six decades. She had an affair with fellow actor Spencer Tracy for almost 30 years. She died at age 96 in 2003, and famously said, "If you obey all the rules, you miss all the fun." She shares a last name with another Hollywood icon, Audrey, even though the two had no relation. What was her name?

24. She is legendary American actress and singer who won an Oscar, an Emmy, and a Tony. She was the mother of the Star Wars actress and writer Carrie Fisher. She is a Hollywood Golden Age icon, who is best known for her role as Kathy Selden in Singin' in the Rain. Other films include The Affairs of Dobie Gillis, Susan Slept Here, Bundle of Joy, and Tammy and the Bachelor. She was embroiled in a major scandal when her husband Eddie Fischer left her for Elizabeth Taylor. On December 28, 2016, she died one day after the death of her daughter Carrie Fisher.

25. He was a British novelist and journalist whose most notable works are Nineteen Eighty-Four, a dystopian story about a world being run by a super state which controls people's lives, people are watched by Big Brother, and individualism is considered a crime. His other notable work is the novella Animal Farm, which is about the years before the 1917 revolution in Russia. He died in 1950. What was this writer's name?

26. He was an American novelist and journalist who is considered one of the greatest American writers of the 20th century. He wrote books like The Sun Also Rises, For Whom the Bell Tolls, and The Old Man and the Sea. He was also a war correspondent who travelled the world on assignments, including the Spanish Civil War in 1937. He won a Pulitzer Prize for Fiction and a Nobel Prize in Literature. In his later years, he lived in Cuba, and he died in 1961 of an apparent suicide. What is this novelist's name?

Answers to Bonus Questions 2:
Notable People in History

1. Amelia Earhart

2. George VI

3. Louis XVI

4. Napoléon Bonaparte

5. Tsar Nicholas II

6. Nefertiti

7. Potiphar or Potifar

8. Victoria

9. Cecil John Rhodes

10. Anne Boleyn

11. Genghis Khan

12. Shaka Zulu

13. Wolfgang Mozart

14. Ludwig van Beethoven

15. Yves Saint Laurent

16. James Brown

17. Thomas Edison

18. Roald Dahl

19. Enid Blyton

20. Sir Elton John

21. John Wesley

22. Pope John Paul II

23. Katharine Hepburn

24. Debbie Reynolds

25. George Orwell

26. Ernest Hemingway

DON'T FORGET YOUR FREE BOOKS

GET THEM FOR FREE ON
WWW.TRIVIABILL.COM

MORE BOOKS BY BILL O'NEILL

I hope you enjoyed this book and learned something new. Please feel free to check out some of my previous books on **Amazon**.

Printed in Great Britain
by Amazon